First World War
and Army of Occupation
War Diary
France, Belgium and Germany

32 DIVISION
96 Infantry Brigade
Northumberland Fusiliers
16th Battalion
22 November 1915 - 7 February 1918

WO95/2398/1

The Naval & Military Press Ltd
www.nmarchive.com
Published in association with The National Archives

Published by

The Naval & Military Press Ltd

Unit 10 Ridgewood Industrial Park,

Uckfield, East Sussex,

TN22 5QE England

Tel: +44 (0) 1825 749494

www.naval-military-press.com

www.nmarchive.com

This diary has been reprinted in facsimile from the original. Any imperfections are inevitably reproduced and the quality may fall short of modern type and cartographic standards.

© **Crown Copyright**
Images reproduced by permission of The National Archives, London, England, 2015.

Contents

Document type	Place/Title	Date From	Date To
Heading	WO95/2398/1		
Heading	32nd Division 96th Infy Bde 16th Bn North'D Fus. Nov 1915-Feb 1918 Disbanded		
Heading	32nd Div 16th North D Fus Vol I Nov-Dec 15		
War Diary	Codford	22/11/1915	23/11/1915
War Diary	Boulogne	24/11/1915	24/11/1915
War Diary	Domqueur	27/11/1915	27/11/1915
War Diary	Bourdon	28/11/1915	28/11/1915
War Diary	Cardonette	30/11/1915	30/11/1915
War Diary	Meaulte	30/11/1915	20/12/1915
War Diary	F. 2	21/12/1915	31/12/1915
Heading	96th Brigade. 32nd Division. 16th Battalion Northumberland Fusiliers January 1916		
Heading	16th Northumb Fus. Vol.2 Jan 16		
War Diary	Millencourt	01/01/1916	02/01/1916
War Diary	Martinsart	03/01/1916	06/01/1916
War Diary	G 2	07/01/1916	10/01/1916
War Diary	Millencourt	13/01/1916	17/01/1916
War Diary	G. 2	18/01/1916	21/01/1916
War Diary	Authville	22/01/1916	31/01/1916
Heading	96th Brigade. 32nd Division. 16th Battalion Northumberland Fusiliers February 1916		
War Diary	Millencourt	01/02/1916	05/02/1916
War Diary	Martinsart	06/02/1916	13/02/1916
War Diary	Millencourt	14/02/1916	24/02/1916
War Diary	Aveluy	25/02/1916	29/02/1916
Heading	96th Brigade. 32nd Division. 16th Battalion Northumberland Fusiliers March 1916		
Heading	16 Northumb Fus Vol 4		
War Diary	Aveluy	01/03/1916	08/03/1916
War Diary	Bouzincourt	09/03/1916	12/03/1916
War Diary	F G 2	13/03/1916	16/03/1916
War Diary	Authville	17/03/1916	20/03/1916
War Diary	F. G. 2	20/03/1916	24/03/1916
War Diary	Bouzincourt	25/03/1916	31/03/1916
Heading	96th Brigade 32nd Division. 16th Battalion Northumberland Fusiliers April 1916		
War Diary	F. 9. 2 Subsector	01/04/1916	03/04/1916
War Diary	Bouzincourt	04/04/1916	04/04/1916
War Diary	Pierregot	05/04/1916	23/04/1916
War Diary	Senlis	24/04/1916	24/04/1916
War Diary	Authville	25/04/1916	28/04/1916
War Diary	Authville Sector	29/04/1916	30/04/1916
Heading	96th Brigade. 32nd Division. 16th Battalion Northumberland Fusiliers May 1916		
Miscellaneous	A Form. Messages And Signals.		
War Diary	Authville Sector.	01/05/1916	02/05/1916
War Diary	Aveluy	03/05/1916	13/05/1916
War Diary	Warloy	14/05/1916	17/05/1916
War Diary	Contay Wood	18/05/1916	29/05/1916

War Diary	Aveluy Wood	30/05/1916	30/05/1916
War Diary	Thiepval Subsector	31/05/1916	31/05/1916
Heading	96th Brigade. 32nd Division. 1/16th Battalion Northumberland Fusiliers June 1916		
War Diary	Thiepval Subsector	01/06/1916	03/06/1916
War Diary	Black Horse Bridge	04/06/1916	07/06/1916
War Diary	Thiepval Subsector	08/06/1916	13/06/1916
War Diary	Warloy	14/06/1916	30/06/1916
Heading	96th Inf. Bde. 32nd Div. War Diary 16th Battn. The Northumberland Fusiliers. July 1916		
Heading	War Diary 16th Northumberland Fusiliers 1st July 1916-31st July 1916 Vol 8		
War Diary	Thiepval Sector	01/07/1916	01/07/1916
War Diary	'Bluff'	01/07/1916	01/07/1916
War Diary	Aveluy Wood	02/07/1916	03/07/1916
War Diary	Warloy	04/07/1916	05/07/1916
War Diary	Lealvillers	06/07/1916	08/07/1916
War Diary	Senlis	09/07/1916	11/07/1916
War Diary	Ovillers	12/07/1916	14/07/1916
War Diary	Bouzincourt	15/07/1916	15/07/1916
War Diary	Warloy	16/07/1916	16/07/1916
War Diary	Beauval	17/07/1916	17/07/1916
War Diary	Neuvillette	18/07/1916	19/07/1916
War Diary	Blangerval	20/07/1916	20/07/1916
War Diary	Anvin	27/07/1916	27/07/1916
War Diary	Fontain-Les-Hermans	22/07/1916	26/07/1916
War Diary	Labeuvriere	26/07/1916	28/07/1916
War Diary	Houchin	29/07/1916	31/07/1916
Heading	96th Brigade. 32nd Division. 16th Battalion Northumberland Fusiliers August 1916		
Heading	War Diary 16th Northd Fusrs From 1st August 1916 to 31st August 1916 Vol 9		
War Diary	Houchin	01/08/1916	05/08/1916
War Diary	Bethune	06/08/1916	19/08/1916
War Diary	Cambrin Left Sub Sector	21/08/1916	24/08/1916
War Diary	Cambrin Village Line	25/08/1916	28/08/1916
War Diary	Cambrin Left Sub Sector	29/08/1916	31/08/1916
Heading	96th Brigade. 32nd Division. 16th Battalion Northumberland Fusiliers September 1916		
Heading	War Diary of 16th (Service) Battalion, Northumberland Fusiliers. from 1st September 1916 to 30th September 1916. (Volume 10)		
War Diary		01/09/1916	01/09/1916
War Diary	Annequin	02/09/1916	05/09/1916
War Diary	Cambrin Left Sub-Section	06/09/1916	09/09/1916
War Diary	Cambrin (Village Line)	10/09/1916	13/09/1916
War Diary	Cambrin (Left Subsection)	14/09/1916	17/09/1916
War Diary	Beuvry	18/09/1916	25/09/1916
War Diary	Cuinchy (Support Line)	26/09/1916	29/09/1916
War Diary	Cuinchy (Right Sub-Section)	30/09/1916	30/09/1916
Heading	Diary 16 Northd Fus Sept, 1916		
Heading	96th Brigade. 32nd Division. 16th Battalion Northumberland Fusiliers. October 1916		
Heading	16th (S) Bn Northumberland Fusiliers War Diary Period 1-31st October 1916 Volume 11		
War Diary	Cuinchy Right-Sub-Section	01/10/1916	03/10/1916

War Diary	Le Quesnoy	04/10/1916	07/10/1916
War Diary	Cuinchy Right-Sub-Section	08/10/1916	10/10/1916
War Diary	Bethune	11/10/1916	14/10/1916
War Diary	Dieval	15/10/1916	15/10/1916
War Diary	Frevillers	16/10/1916	16/10/1916
War Diary	Gouy-En-Ternois.	17/10/1916	17/10/1916
War Diary	Amplier	18/10/1916	18/10/1916
War Diary	Harponville	21/10/1916	22/10/1916
War Diary	Brickfields	23/10/1916	23/10/1916
War Diary	Albert	23/10/1916	25/10/1916
War Diary	Warloy	26/10/1916	30/10/1916
War Diary	Herissart	31/10/1916	31/10/1916
Heading	96th Brigade. 32nd Division. 16th Battalion Northumberland Fusiliers November 1916		
Heading	War Diary. 16th Northumberland Fusiliers. From November 1st to 30th. 1916. Vol 12		
War Diary	Herissart	01/11/1916	12/11/1916
War Diary	Warloy	13/11/1916	13/11/1916
War Diary	Schwaben Redoubt	14/11/1916	16/11/1916
War Diary	Mailly Maillet	17/11/1916	18/11/1916
War Diary	Ellis Square	19/11/1916	19/11/1916
War Diary	K 35.45.65.10	20/11/1916	20/11/1916
War Diary	K 35.54.82. E	20/11/1916	20/11/1916
War Diary	K 35.73.70	20/11/1916	20/11/1916
War Diary	K 35c.45.65 E	21/11/1916	21/11/1916
War Diary	K 35c 54.82. E	21/11/1916	21/11/1916
War Diary	K 35c.73.70 E	21/11/1916	21/11/1916
War Diary	K 35d.50.60	21/11/1916	23/11/1916
War Diary	Rainecheval	24/11/1916	24/11/1916
War Diary	Amplier	25/11/1916	25/11/1916
War Diary	Bonneville	26/11/1916	30/11/1916
Heading	96th Brigade. 32nd Division. 16th Battalion Northumberland Fusiliers December 1916		
Heading	War Diary Of 16th (Service) Bn. Northumberland Fusiliers From 1st December 1916 To 31st December Vol 13		
War Diary	Bonneville	01/12/1916	31/12/1916
Heading	War Diary Of 16th Bn. Northumberland Fusiliers. From 1st January 1917. To 31st January 1917. Vol. 14		
War Diary	Bonneville	01/01/1917	05/01/1917
War Diary	Sarton	06/01/1917	06/01/1917
War Diary	Bus And Couin	07/01/1917	07/01/1917
War Diary	Bus	08/01/1917	13/01/1917
War Diary	C 4	14/01/1917	15/01/1917
War Diary	Courcelles	16/01/1917	18/01/1917
War Diary	K 35.c.3.2 to K 35.a.45.95	19/01/1917	21/01/1917
War Diary	Bertrancourt	22/01/1917	25/01/1917
War Diary	C 3	26/01/1917	27/01/1917
War Diary	Mailly-Maillet	28/01/1917	31/01/1917
Heading	War Diary Of 16th (S) Bn. Northumberland Fusiliers From 1st February 1917 To 28th February 1917. Vol. 15		
War Diary	Mailly Maillet	01/02/1917	01/02/1917
War Diary	R 3 Subsector	02/02/1917	13/02/1917
War Diary	Lealvillers	14/02/1917	15/02/1917
War Diary	Contay	16/02/1917	16/02/1917

War Diary	Villers-Bocage	17/02/1917	19/02/1917
War Diary	Camon	20/02/1917	20/02/1917
War Diary	Berteaucourt	21/02/1917	22/02/1917
War Diary	Fresnoy	23/02/1917	23/02/1917
War Diary	Beaufort	24/02/1917	26/02/1917
War Diary	G.B.5. To G.B.1	27/02/1917	28/02/1917
Heading	War Diary. Of 16th (S) Bn. Northumberland Fusiliers. From 1st March 1917. To 31st March 1917. Vol. 16		
War Diary	Beaufort	01/03/1917	07/03/1917
War Diary	Le Quesnoy	08/03/1917	13/03/1917
War Diary	Bouchoir	14/03/1917	18/03/1917
War Diary	Voyennes	19/03/1917	20/03/1917
War Diary	Offoy	21/03/1917	28/03/1917
War Diary	Matigny	29/03/1917	30/03/1917
War Diary	Germaine	31/03/1917	31/03/1917
Heading	War Diary. Of 16th Bn. Northumberland Fusiliers. From 1st April 1917. To 30th April 1917. Vol. 17		
War Diary		01/04/1917	11/04/1917
War Diary	Germaine	12/04/1917	14/04/1917
War Diary	Fayet	15/04/1917	16/04/1917
War Diary	Holnon	17/04/1917	20/04/1917
War Diary	Germaine	20/04/1917	20/04/1917
War Diary	Athies	21/04/1917	30/04/1917
Heading	War Diary Of 16th (S) Bn. Northumberland Fusiliers From 1st May 1917. To 31st May 1917 Vol. XVIII.		
War Diary	Athies	01/05/1917	16/05/1917
War Diary	Omiecourt	16/05/1917	16/05/1917
War Diary	Rosieres	17/05/1917	29/05/1917
War Diary	Guillaucourt	30/05/1917	31/05/1917
Heading	War Diary Of 16th (S) Bn. Northumberland Fusiliers From 1st June 1917. To 30th June 1917. Vol XIX.		
War Diary	Bleu	01/06/1917	11/06/1917
War Diary	Steenvorde	12/06/1917	12/06/1917
War Diary	Wormhoudt	13/06/1917	14/06/1917
War Diary	Malo-Bains	15/06/1917	22/06/1917
War Diary	Coxyde	23/06/1917	24/06/1917
War Diary	Ghyvelde	25/06/1917	30/06/1917
Heading	War Diary Of 16th (S) Bn. Northumberland Fusiliers, From 1st July 1917 To 31st July 1917. Vol. XX.		
War Diary	Ghyvelde	01/07/1917	04/07/1917
War Diary	Nieuport.	05/07/1917	31/07/1917
Heading	War Diary Of 16th Bn. Northumberland Fusiliers. From 1st August, 1917 to 31st August 1917 Vol. XXI.		
War Diary	Coxyde	01/08/1917	01/08/1917
War Diary	Oost Dunkerke	02/08/1917	03/08/1917
War Diary	Trenches St. Georges Left Subsector	04/08/1917	08/08/1917
War Diary	Trenches St. Georges Sub-Sector (Left)	08/08/1917	09/08/1917
War Diary	Ribaillet Camp	10/08/1917	17/08/1917
War Diary	Coxyde	18/08/1917	18/08/1917
War Diary	Bray Dunes	19/08/1917	29/08/1917
War Diary	Coxyde	30/08/1917	31/08/1917
Heading	War Diary Of 16th (S) Bn. Northumberland Fusiliers. Vol XXII.		
War Diary	Coxyde	01/09/1917	11/09/1917
War Diary	Lombartzyde Right Sub. Sector E. of Canal	12/09/1917	16/09/1917
War Diary	Nieuport	17/09/1917	20/09/1917

War Diary	Lombartzyde Right Sub. Sect. E. of Canal.	21/09/1917	23/09/1917
War Diary	Nieuport.	24/09/1917	27/09/1917
War Diary	Coxyde	28/09/1917	30/09/1917
Heading	16 North D Fus. War Diary. 1st To 30th Sept 17. Vol XXII		
Heading	War Diary Of 16th Bn. Northumberland Fusiliers 1st to 31st October 1917. Vol XXIII		
War Diary	Coxyde	01/10/1917	02/10/1917
War Diary	La Panne	03/10/1917	05/10/1917
War Diary	Fort Des Dunes.	06/10/1917	24/10/1917
War Diary	Teteghem	25/10/1917	25/10/1917
War Diary	Zeggers Cappel	26/10/1917	31/10/1917
Heading	War Diary Of 16th Bn. Northumberland Fusiliers 1st To 30th November 1917. Vol XXIV		
Miscellaneous	A Form. Messages And Signals.		
War Diary	Zeggers Cappel	01/11/1917	11/11/1917
War Diary	Ledringhem	12/11/1917	12/11/1917
War Diary	Sheet 27. J.7.a.16	13/11/1917	13/11/1917
War Diary	Turco Farm	14/11/1917	23/11/1917
War Diary	Brake Camp	24/11/1917	28/11/1917
War Diary	Wurst Farm	29/11/1917	30/11/1917
Heading	War Diary Of 16th Bn. Northumberland Fusiliers. 1st To 31st December 1917. Volume XXV.		
Heading	War Diary Of 16th Bn. Northumberland Fusiliers 1st to 31st December 1917. Volume XXV		
War Diary		01/12/1917	31/12/1917
Heading	War Diary Of 16th Bn. Northumberland Fusiliers 1st To 31st January, 1918. Vol XXVI		
War Diary	Sanghen	01/01/1918	31/01/1918
Heading	War Diary. Of 16th Bn. Northumberland Fusiliers 1st to 7th February 1918. Volume XXVII		
War Diary	Egypt House	01/02/1918	02/02/1918
War Diary	Abricamp	03/02/1918	05/02/1918
War Diary	Larry Camp	06/02/1918	07/02/1918

WO 95/23981

32ND DIVISION
96TH INFY BDE

16TH BN NORTH'D FUS.

NOV 1915 - FEB 1918

DISBANDED

16½ Nathaniel & Thos:
tot. I
Nov–Dec '15
131/7936

16th Bn. NORTH'D FUSILIERS.

Army Form C. 2118

WAR DIARY
or
INTELLIGENCE SUMMARY

(Erase heading not required.)

Instructions regarding War Diaries and Intelligence Summaries are contained in F.S. Regs., Part II. and the Staff Manual respectively. Title Pages will be prepared in manuscript.

Place	Date	Hour	Summary of Events and Information	Remarks and references to Appendices
CODFORD	22/11/15	3.30am	Transport, Signallers, M.S., O.R.S, Cooks, M.G. Section proceeded to FRANCE via CODFORD-SOUTHAMPTON-HAVRE.	
	23/11/15		Remainder of the Battalion proceeded to FRANCE via FOLKESTONE-BOULOGNE. On arrival at BOULOGNE the Battalion proceeded to the rest camp at OSTROHOVE.	
BOULOGNE	24/11/15	8.20am	Battalion entrained at GARE CENTRALE, BOULOGNE and proceeded to LONGPRÉ where it detrained and marched to DOMQUEUR. The advance party of the Battalion arrived at DOMQUEUR from HAVRE on the 24th November. Three Companies were billeted in DOMQUEUR and one in LE PLOUY.	
DOMQUEUR	27/11/15		The Battalion proceeded to BOURDON where it was billeted for the night.	
BOURDON	28/11/15		The Battalion proceeded to CARDONETTE.	
CARDONETTE	30/11/15		The Battalion proceeded to MÉAULTE. Half billeted in MÉAULTE, half billeted in BERNANCOURT.	

WAR DIARY or INTELLIGENCE SUMMARY

Army Form C. 2118

Place	Date	Hour	Summary of Events and Information	Remarks and references to Appendices
MÉAULTE	30/11/15		A Battalion attached to 54th Infantry Brigade for training.	
	1/12/15		Half the officers and half the N.C.O.'s proceeded to Lectures D1 and D2 occupied by the 1st BEDFORDSHIRE Regt. and 11th ROYAL FUSILIERS respectively for individual training in trench warfare.	
	2/12/15		Remaining half of the officers and N.C.O.'s proceeded as above for individual training in trench warfare.	
	3/12/15		One Platoon per company proceeded to Lectures D1 and D2 for 48 hours training in trench warfare.	
	5/12/15		The remaining Platoons proceeded to Lectures D1 and D2 for 48 hours training in trench warfare. The 6th NORTHANTS relieved the 11th R.F. in Lectr D2 on the 4th Dec/15	
	7/12/15		Company training commenced. A Coy took over Right Sector of D1 and B Coy Right Sector of D1 from 4 & 8 towers.	
	9/12/15		D Coy took over Right Sector of D2 and C Coy Right Sector of D1 from 49 towers—	

WAR DIARY
or
INTELLIGENCE SUMMARY
(Erase heading not required.)

Army Form C. 2118

Instructions regarding War Diaries and Intelligence Summaries are contained in F. S. Regs., Part II. and the Staff Manual respectively. Title Pages will be prepared in manuscript.

Place	Date	Hour	Summary of Events and Information	Remarks and references to Appendices
	11/12/15		Battalion less D Coy. relieved by Northants in trenches D.2.	
	15/12/15		Nothing of any importance occurred during our tour of duty in the trenches. Relieved and in rest 15th Dec. in billets in ALBERT. The Battn. was relieved by the 11th R.F.	
	24/12/15		Between the 15th and today the Battn. being in Divisional Reserve manned R.E. fatigues each day. A. & B. Coys proceeded to the trenches left of E.2 on the 19th & D Coy to relieve two Coys of the 7th BERKSHIRE Regt. On the 20th Dec. the remainder of the Battalion proceeded to E.2 to relieve the remainder of the BERKSHIRE Regt.	
E.2	24/12/15		Situation normal. A.G. + minenwerfer active but were silenced. Trenches in a very bad condition in right sector. Working party seen opposite trenches 114 at 7.30 a.m. but disappeared when fired upon.	

1875 Wt. W593/826 1,000,000 4/15 J.B.C. & A. A.D.S.S./Forms/C.2118.

WAR DIARY
or
INTELLIGENCE SUMMARY

(Erase heading not required.)

Army Form C. 2118

Place	Date	Hour	Summary of Events and Information	Remarks and references to Appendices
	22/6/15		Situation normal. No working parties were sent, probably due to full moon. Distribution of Coys. Right Sector, B Coy; Right Centre "C" Coy; Centre "A" Coy; Reserve Coy D Coy.	
	23/6/15		Situation normal. No different seen in enemy works. A small party repairing new German section 119 but discontinued as soon as we fired. Ye enemy shelled ALBERT between 9-11 pm & threw a few shells between 19-12 am on our lines. Shelled by our artillery. Quiet all other times. Enemy's snipers very active. Enemy has burned at stand to, 5.30 p.m. in direction of LA BOISSELLE. Entries upon that a bomb & dummy were thrown right of 21.4 & 22.10 and from GERMAN lines. Work on the trenches is being continued & considerable improvement has been made.	
	24/6/15		Situation normal. Enemy aero-plane communication trench opposite L.Sn 113 between front line & support line working towards each other. Flare was slipped M.G. & snipers fire.	

WAR DIARY
or
INTELLIGENCE SUMMARY
(Erase heading not required.)

Army Form C. 2118

Instructions regarding War Diaries and Intelligence Summaries are contained in F. S. Regs., Part II. and the Staff Manual respectively. Title Pages will be prepared in manuscript.

Place	Date	Hour	Summary of Events and Information	Remarks and references to Appendices
	25/7/16		Situation normal. Very little doing in either side. No % was sent in to GERMAN lines as if they were holding in contact, other sectors 113–116. Dugout parties continued to clear trenches.	
	26/7/16		Situation normal. GERMAN artillery shelled BÉCOURT at intervals during the day but was silenced by our artillery.	
	27/7/16		Situation normal. Disposition of bays Right sector A by, left sector D by, support B by, reserve C by. Enemy artillery fairly active but caused less than our artillery replied	
	27/7/16		Quiet. A few shells over BÉCOURT, no damage. Entirety of drain trenches, few improvements made.	
	28/7/16		Situation normal. M.G. & snipers still continue to fire from the althou'h they have been repeatedly shelled by our own. Mine was exploded in the ILOT at 3·20 p.m. which was	

WAR DIARY
or
INTELLIGENCE SUMMARY
(Erase heading not required.)

Army Form C. 2118

Place	Date	Hour	Summary of Events and Information	Remarks and references to Appendices
	29/12/15		followed immediately by enemys T.M. Our artillery retaliated. The Battalion was relieved by the 10th ESSEX Regt. and we	
	30/12/15		proceeded to MELUNCOURT. Resting in billets.	
	31/12/15		Resting in billets.	

31.12.15 ① ec/15.

W H Ritson
Lt. Col.
Commdg. 16th Bn. N.F.

96th Brigade.
32nd Division.

16th BATTALION

NORTHUMBERLAND FUSILIERS

JANUARY 1916

16ᵗʰ Instrument = Two:
Vol: 2
7 AV 16

96/32.

16th Bn Northumberland Fusiliers

WAR DIARY
INTELLIGENCE SUMMARY

Army Form C. 2118

Place	Date	Hour	Summary of Events and Information	Remarks and references to Appendices
MILLENCOURT	1/1/16		Resting in billets. A special dinner was prepared for the men which was served to them in billets owing to lack of accommodation. All the officers dined together for the first time since we left England.	
	2/1/16		Battalion less 3 officers and 100 other ranks proceeded to MARTINSART as Divisional Reserve. 3 officers and 100 other ranks proceeded to Forward MOUND KEEP.	
MARTINSART	3/1/16		Worked on MARTINSART defences and generally cleaned up billets and drained and repaired roads.	
	4/1/16		Carried on with work commenced on the 3rd Jany. The C.O. and Adjt. proceeded to C.9.2 Labenster to make arrangements with 2nd ROYAL INNISKILLING FUSILIERS as relieving them on 6th January.	
	5/1/16		Carried on with work commenced on the 3rd.	
	6/1/16		Battalion proceeded to C.9.2 Labenster at 3:30 p.m. to relieve 2nd ROYAL INNISKILLING FUSILIERS. Relief satisfactorily completed by 7:45 p.m. Casualties nil.	
C.2.	7/1/16		During the night everything was very quiet over the whole line. "B" Coy reported tapping was heard between midnight and 2 a.m. in HAMMERHEAD Sap. Brigade informed and one of mining experts to	

WAR DIARY or INTELLIGENCE SUMMARY

Place	Date	Hour	Summary of Events and Information	Remarks and references to Appendices
	9/1/16		Very little rifle or M.G. fire. Casualties nil. Everything very quiet early morning but at 4.30 am enemy's artillery fired about 20 shells over trench 155. No damage done. We could not get any retaliation from our guns as they had not finished registering. Minny report listened several times at HAMMERHEAD tip but did not hear anything. Enemy's artillery active all day. Our guns replied but only feebly. Enemy sent over 10 emisties. Our T.M.B. silenced them. Very little rifle or M.G. fire. Wind N.W. Casualties, 1 killed, 1 died of wounds, 5 wounded.	
	9/1/16		Situation unchanged, very quiet. All boys went out mining parties who were successful in carrying out some good work without interruption. Artillery sent over about 5 whizzbangs over French 155 but were silenced by our guns. Very little rifle & M.G. fire. Wind N.W. Casualties nil.	
	10/1/16		Enemy fired several emisties yesterday afternoon and evening behind 151, 152 and from new 154 - 156. 0 a fell in a dugout burying four men in "B" bay. They were quickly dug out and were none the	

WAR DIARY
or
INTELLIGENCE SUMMARY

(Erase heading not required.)

Army Form C. 2118

Place	Date	Hour	Summary of Events and Information	Remarks and references to Appendices
MILLENCOURT	13/1/16 14/1/16 15/1/16 16/1/16		more except for slight shock. Our artillery retaliated fully. The artillery town has been of very great assistance to us during this tour of duty in the trenches, but as they have just come out and their first time behind the line allowances must be made for them. Sgt MAIR "A" Coy, reports that he noticed new timber in enemys trench N.N.E of MAISON GRISE SAP. He observed someone apparently directing others. He fired and saw the man fall. 2 enemy's Snipers were heard in direction of ST. PIERRE DIVION. This was reported to artillery officer who enquired and found two salvoes at 7.45 p.m and 8.30 p.m. Very little rifle or M.G. fire. The Battalion was relieved by the 15th Bn. H.L.I. The relief commenced at 6.30 p.m and was completed at 8.30 p.m. The Battalion proceeded by Platoons to MILLENCOURT trod Platoon arriving at 12.15 a.m. Casualties nil. Battalion carried on under Coy arrangements, made kitmes drill, bombing etc	

WAR DIARY
or
INTELLIGENCE SUMMARY
(Erase heading not required.)

Army Form C. 2118

Place	Date	Hour	Summary of Events and Information	Remarks and references to Appendices
	17/9/16		The Battalion was inspected by His Grace the Duke of Northumberland, K.G. The Duke was accompanied by Capt. NAPIER, Secretary of the Northumberland Association, which Association had invited His Grace to come out to inspect the Territorial Bns. of the Northd. Fusiliers. There were also present officers from the 3rd Army, 32nd Division and the Staff of the 96th Infantry Brigade. On its arrival the Bn. was drawn up in review order. He inspected them and then the Bn. marched past. His Grace made a short speech in which he mentioned that the last time he inspected the Battalion was on the pastures at ALNWICK and that he was pleased as he was to have had the opportunity of inspecting it again in France. He also complimented the Bn. upon its smart appearance. A letter was received from the Brigadier and also one from the Staff Captain expressing their great satisfaction at the smartness of the whole parade. The C.O. was laid up with a bad throat and unable to attend the parade. In his absence Major Little took command.	

WAR DIARY or INTELLIGENCE SUMMARY

Army Form C. 2118

Place	Date	Hour	Summary of Events and Information	Remarks and references to Appendices
Q.2.	18/1/16		The Battalion relieved the 19th Bn. LANCASHIRE FUSILIERS in Q.2 Sector. First Platoon left MILLENCOURT at 3.30 p.m. and proceeded via ALBERT-AVELUY-AUTHUILLE. The relief was satisfactorily completed by 8 p.m. Disposition of Coys. from right to left C,D,A,B. In the absence of the C.O. who was wounded to Hospital in the morning, Major LITTLE took command of the Bn. with Major KREMER as 2nd in command. Casualties nil.	
	19/1/16		Everything very quiet during the night. Our artillery strafed line at trench plan R.25.b.13.6 R.25.b.2.9. The bombardment started at 11.50 a.m. and lasted 35 minutes. As far as could be judged a lot of damage was done both to front line and support trenches. It was a Divisional bombardment and about 70 shells were fired. Enemy retaliation was exceedingly feeble. A patrol under 2/Lt PROCTOR to make a reconnaissance of the sunken road from PETERHEAD SAP at 10.35 p.m. under the enemy wire and the patrol returned at 12.15 a.m. No signs of enemy and much too light for successful work.	

WAR DIARY or INTELLIGENCE SUMMARY

Army Form C. 2118

Place	Date	Hour	Summary of Events and Information	Remarks and references to Appendices
	20/1/16		About 5.30 a.m. a German working party of about 60 men were seen at R.19.c.7.4. - R.19.c.10.1. It was fired on by M.G. and not seen again during the night. It was not possible to estimate the damage done. Casualties. 3 other ranks wounded. Wind. S.W. Both sides very quiet during the night and the greater part of the day. The enemy sent over a few small shells about 2 a.m. We retaliated with 4 howrs. and 12 18 pounders. There was occasional shelling of other parts of the day but no damage was done. Lt FALCONER and Capt. THOMPSON went out on patrol from Sap 37 at 1.30 a.m. The objective was the crossroads at R.25.d.4.7. They crossed the mire with little difficulty and proceeded on to where and wounded their way to crossroads. A good deal of information was gained about the condition of ground etc., but no signs of the enemy or their work were discovered. The progress of the patrol was impeded by M.G. fire and the brightness of the night which was again moonlight. The patrol returned via HAMMERHEAD SAP at 3.45 a.m.	

Army Form C. 2118

WAR DIARY
or
INTELLIGENCE SUMMARY
(Erase heading not required.)

Instructions regarding War Diaries and Intelligence Summaries are contained in F.S. Regs., Part II. and the Staff Manual respectively. Title Pages will be prepared in manuscript.

Place	Date	Hour	Summary of Events and Information	Remarks and references to Appendices
	21/1/16		W. McLEAN together with a Sergt. and a private left PETERHEAD SAP at 10.30p.m. and endeavoured to the sunken road. No signs of the enemy were discovered. Casualties, other ranks two. Very fine day and very quiet. The Battalion was relieved by the 2nd Bn. ROYAL INNISKILLING FUSILIERS the relief commencing at 5.30 p.m. It was satisfactorily completed at 7.15 p.m. The Battalion less two Platoons B Coy who arrived GORDON CASTLE, proceeded to billets and dugouts at AUTHUILLE as Brigade Reserve.	
AUTHUILLE	22/1/16		Casualties nil. Provided R.E. fatigues.	
	23/1/16		Divisional and troop guns shelled "THIEPVAL" at 4.45 p.m. from 30 rounds, 115 rounds. Enemy retaliated on AVELUY and AUTHUILLE with several salvos, no damage done. Casualties nil. Provided R.E. fatigues.	
	24/1/16		do.	
	25/1/16		do.	

WAR DIARY or INTELLIGENCE SUMMARY

Army Form C. 2118

Place	Date	Hour	Summary of Events and Information	Remarks and references to Appendices
	26/1/16		The Battalion was relieved by the 19th Bn. LANCASHIRE FUSILIERS. Relief was timed to commence at 6 p.m. but first Platoon of LANCS. did not arrive until 7.30 p.m. Relief was satisfactorily completed by 8.20 p.m. Battalion moved back to MILLENCOURT by Platoons and took over the old billets.	
	27/1/16		Day spent in cleaning up equipment, arms etc.	
	28/1/16		Fatigue party sent to BOUZINCOURT for work on the intermediate line. Wiring party under Capt. DUNGLINSON and Lt. WAKE were practiced in erecting a wire apron fence both during the day and at night. This is for the scheme to be carried out in F. Sector. A dipping party under Lt. AVERY and Lt. WATSON of 100 other ranks was also practiced in dipping. This is also in connection with the F sector scheme. Battalion found fatigues.	
	29/1/16		Wiring party was out both during the day and at night. Fatigues. Brigadier inspected all the Brigade wiring parties at a place on the	
	30/1/16		BOUZINCOURT — MILLENCOURT road. Lt. AVERY was evacuated to Hospital on the 29th. In consequence Lt. R.W. FALCONER has been detailed to take command of dipping party.	

Army Form C. 2118

WAR DIARY
or
INTELLIGENCE SUMMARY
(Erase heading not required.)

Instructions regarding War Diaries and Intelligence Summaries are contained in F.S. Regs., Part II. and the Staff Manual respectively. Title Pages will be prepared in manuscript.

Place	Date	Hour	Summary of Events and Information	Remarks and references to Appendices
	31/1/16		Battalion found fatigues. Very heavy firing East & the south of MILLENCOURT. Battalion retired to stand-to at 5.50 pm and was ready to march off within half an hour. Orders to stand down received at 8.15 pm.	
	31/1/16		Arthur W. Little Major, Commdg. 16th Bn. Northd. Fusiliers.	

96th Brigade.
32nd Division.

16th BATTALION

NORTHUMBERLAND FUSILIERS

FEBRUARY 1916

1st Bn. NORTHUMBERLAND FUSILIERS.

WAR DIARY
or
INTELLIGENCE SUMMARY

Army Form C. 2118

(Erase heading not required.)

Instructions regarding War Diaries and Intelligence Summaries are contained in F. S. Regs., Part II. and the Staff Manual respectively. Title Pages will be prepared in manuscript.

Place	Date	Hour	Summary of Events and Information	Remarks and references to Appendices
MILLENCOURT	1/2/16		Battalion provided working parties.	
	2/2/16		Battalion provided working parties. Wiring and digging parties provided to F. sector to carry out the scheme of strong-points in front of the sector. The work was satisfactorily carried out and without casualties. 2nd Lt. J.H. GREEN. transferred from R.F.C. reported for duty and was posted to "B" Coy.	
	3/2/16		Digging party provided to F. sector to carry on with work commenced the previous night. Battalion rested during the day.	
	4/2/16		Digging party proceeded to F sector to carry on with work commenced on 2nd Feby. 2nd Lt. C.H. PURCHASE, commissioned from H.A.C., reported for duty on 3rd Feby and was posted to "A" Coy.	
	5/2/16		Battalion provided working parties. 2nd Lt. H.F. WHITE, commissioned from the ARGYLL and SUTHERLAND HIGHLANDERS, reported for duty and was posted to "C" Coy.	

WAR DIARY

or

INTELLIGENCE SUMMARY

(Erase heading not required.)

Army Form C. 2118

Place	Date	Hour	Summary of Events and Information	Remarks and references to Appendices
MARTINSART	6/2/16		Battalion proceeded to MARTINSART to relieve the 1st DORSETS. "C" Coy provided the parties for AUTHUILLE KEEPS under L. PORTER. "D" Coy provided parties for McMAHONS POST and MILL KEEP under L. SOUTHERN.	
	7/2/16		Battalion provided working parties.	
	8/2/16		do.	
	9/2/16		do.	
	10/2/16		do.	
	11/2/16		do.	
	12/2/16		Lt. J. SOUTHERN wounded the forearm by shrapnel at McMAHONS POST. Lt. J. WATSON was sent to relieve him. A & D Coys were relieved by the 5th WEST YORKS REGT. at 6 P.m. and proceeded to MILLENCOURT.	
	13/2/16		Enemy shelled MARTINSART in the evening, no damage done. H.Qrs and B & C Coys relieved by 4th YORK and LANCS at 6 P.m. and proceeded to MILLENCOURT.	
MILLENCOURT.	14/2/16		Day spent in cleaning up and refitting.	

WAR DIARY
INTELLIGENCE SUMMARY
(Erase heading not required.)

Army Form C. 2118

3.

Place	Date	Hour	Summary of Events and Information	Remarks and references to Appendices
	15/2/16		Battalion route march LAVIEVILLE - BRESLE - BAIZIEUX - HENENCOURT. Men marched exceedingly well.	
	16/2/16		Battalion practised mining, smoke helmet drill etc. It was very wet — impossible to do a great deal outside.	
	17/2/16		Battalion relieved 16th H.L.I. in F2 sector. Relief was completed by 12.30 a.m. One rifleman wounded by infantry, otherwise everything was satisfactory. Disposition of Coys from right to left B, C, — D Coys with A Coy in reserve. Artillery fairly active especially in vicinity of Bn H.Q. but no damage was done. We retaliated at intervals. A very heavy shower by the very wet to the NORTH of us about 1 a.m. and continued at intervals until about 4 a.m. Very little rifle or M.G. fire. Trenches in very bad state of repair, very wet in places making it absolutely necessary to wear gum boots. Hind O.N.H.	
	18/2/16		Considerable artillery activity on the part of the enemy, practically all the shells falling in AUTHUILLE WOOD. Our artillery retaliated but was rather slow.	

Army Form C. 2118

WAR DIARY or INTELLIGENCE SUMMARY
(Erase heading not required.)

Place	Date	Hour	Summary of Events and Information	Remarks and references to Appendices
	19/2/16		Very little rifle or M.G. fire. German M.G. was out of action by H.E. at point X.7.c.90.92. Green flares were sent up at intervals all along enemy line during 7 pm – 8 pm. Nothing occurred to explain this. D' Coy sent out patrol of 1 officer and 5 O.R. went out at 6.45 pm & returned at 7.42 pm consisting of 2 Corporals & left of valley. 2 men went out at 6.45 pm & returned at 7.42 pm, carried on with the clearing of trenches and rebuilding parapets. Wind N.W. Considerable activity on the part of the enemy's artillery was again shown. Battalion H.Q. seems to be a marked spot. Also the dugouts of the reserve Coy. Rifle and M.G. fire was much heavier on both sides than on previous days. An enemy balloon was observed at bearing (True) 93° from X.1.c.60.15. from 9.20 am & 12.50 pm. At 11.30 pm sound of an aeroplane from OVILLERS neared over AUTHUILLE WOOD dropping triple flare (red). Returned at 12 midnight dropping triple flare (green) to own division.	
	20/2/16		Heavy party strengthened wire in front of X.7.c. Artillery on both sides quiet. More rifle and M.G. fire than usual. At 4.45 pm a burst of M.G. fire from enemy X.3.1.d. (NAB) for five minutes and again at 6 pm. Improvement in condition of trenches. Wind N.E.	

Army Form C. 2118

WAR DIARY
or
INTELLIGENCE SUMMARY
(Erase heading not required.)

Place	Date	Hour	Summary of Events and Information	Remarks and references to Appendices
	21/2/16		Heavy fire was heard during the night of 20th/21st from Southerly direction. Occasional shelling by both sides. B.M.Q. is nearly always the mark of the enemy fire. All Trinkets were fired at intervals during the night from same point in front line X.2.c which was followed by 5 minute rapid rifle and M.G. fire. Condition of trenches greatly improved. Wind N.E. 2nd Lt. ROBERTSON of INDIAN CAVALRY reported for duty with Bn for course of instruction.	
	22/2/16		Occasional shelling on B.M.Q. by enemy's artillery. We bombarded FERME du MOUQUET and POZIERES during the day. Head appeared to be retaliation was dumped at Bn.M.Q. Very little rifle or M.G. fire. Weather cold, and snow fell during the morning. Wind N.	
	23/2/16		Artillery fairly quiet on both sides, also M.G. rifle fire. Patrol of 1 Officer, 1 N.C.O. and 3 men left Tr. X16.c.05.36 at 6.45 a.m. to reconnoitre ridge which runs to enemy line at X1.d.00.95. At 7.50 a.m. it returned to same spot and reported marching party at X1.d.51.87. M.G. fired and a Trm was heard. Patrol of 1 Officer and 2 men left Tr. X.7.b.30.60. to examine ground in front - returned to same pt. at 7.50 a.m. Nothing to report. T.M. fired 8 60 lb. Tr. X7.a.92.59. damage unknown. Enemy retaliated with 4 small H.E. Tr. X7.b.40.60. 2 not falling steadily. Wind N.	

Army Form C. 2118

WAR DIARY
or
INTELLIGENCE SUMMARY
(Erase heading not required.)

Place	Date	Hour	Summary of Events and Information	Remarks and references to Appendices
AVELUY	24/2/16		Battalion relieved by 2nd ROYAL INNISKILLING FUSILIERS. Relief satisfactorily completed by noon. Battalion proceeded to billets in AVELUY as Divisional Reserve.	
	25/2/16		Battalion provided working parties for R.E.	
	26/2/16		Battalion provided working parties for R.E. Maj. Gen. R/ECROFT inspected the defences of AVELUY also billets in the village.	
	27/2/16		Battalion provided working parties for R.E.	
	28/2/16		do.	
	29/2/16		do. Very few men have been able to put both this time as they have been continually on fatigue. Heavy shelling was heard to the South between 6 and 7 tonight.	

Arthur W. Tittle
Major
Commanding 16th Bn. Northd. Fus.

96th Brigade.

32nd Division.

16th BATTALION

NORTHUMBERLAND FUSILIERS

MARCH 1 9 1 6

32

16 Northumb
Fus
Vol 4

16th NORTHUMBERLAND FUSILIERS.

Army Form C. 2118

WAR DIARY or INTELLIGENCE SUMMARY

(Erase heading not required.)

Instructions regarding War Diaries and Intelligence Summaries are contained in F. S. Regs., Part II. and the Staff Manual respectively. Title Pages will be prepared in manuscript.

Place	Date	Hour	Summary of Events and Information	Remarks and references to Appendices
AVELUY	1/3/16		Battalion provided working party for R.E.	
	2/3/16		Battalion relieved 2nd ROYAL INNISKILLING FUSILIERS in F2 subsection. Relief was satisfactorily completed by 12.20pm. Enemy fired several shells into CHORLEY STREET during relief and killed one man and wounded seven.	
	3/3/16		Usual rotation of Coys from right to left. D, B, A with C Coy in reserve. Artillery fairly quiet also M.G. and rifle fire. Orders received from 96 bde to shorten line on right of sector and receive 144 & 146 from 4th Bn. DUKE of WELLINGTON'S. 15th LANCASHIRE FUSILIERS took over trenches 136 & 138 from D-B Coys at 2pm. D Coy moved into reserve and B Coy closed up. Reliefs were satisfactorily carried out.	
	4/3/16		Artillery fairly quiet also M.G. and rifle fire. Enemy observation balloon was seen at 570 (five) from M.66.80y's. This balloon descended at 11.30am when a squadron of 7 of our aeroplanes flew over the lines in an easterly direction. Proposed to Bde that telephones and wire should be supplied for use of	

WAR DIARY
or
INTELLIGENCE SUMMARY

(Erase heading not required.)

Army Form C. 2118

Place	Date	Hour	Summary of Events and Information	Remarks and references to Appendices
	4/3/16		Intelligence Officer states he can communicate direct with artillery from O.P. Several men have had to report sick through exposure etc due to severe weather. Owing to the mud the men are sticking it very well. Artillery active. Enemy fired several canisters into the left of our line but did very little damage.	
	5/3/16		A great improvement has been made in the condition of the trenches. Everything very quiet.	
	6/3/16		Orders received from 96th Inf Bde to shorten line in left & to reserve in Sucrerie in rear from QUARRY BRAE STREET & CHOMBENT STREET. Disposition of Coys. From if to left is 1 Platoon D Coy, D Coy, A Coy, 2 Platoons C Coy with remainder of C & D Coys in reserve.	
	7/3/16		Enemy's artillery very active from 9 am to 11 P.M. and again in the afternoon and evening. Small trench fires were lit to N.W. of AUTHUILLE WOOD and practically all the shells were seen in that direction.	
	8/3/16		Everything quiet all day. Battalion was relieved by 2nd Bn. ROYAL INNISKILLING FUSILIERS	

Army Form C. 2118

3.

WAR DIARY
or
INTELLIGENCE SUMMARY
(Erase heading not required.)

Place	Date	Hour	Summary of Events and Information	Remarks and references to Appendices
BOUZINCOURT	9/3/16		Relief commenced at 7.10 p.m. and was satisfactorily completed by 10.15 a.m. Both Lieut. "B" Coy moved to BOUZINCOURT as Brigade Reserve. "B" Coy went into dugouts at CRUCIFIX CORNER. Battalion provided working parties.	
	10/3/16		Every stafford G.I. instructor held by 16th L.F. commencing about 11 p.m. Bde moved us to "stand to" about 11.30 pm and then orders to "stand to" and move for word in quick succession. The Bn moved off at 12.20 am and arrived at rendezvous H10 d.6.3. at 1.20 a.m. Heavy firing ceased about the time we moved off from BOUZINCOURT and we received orders from Brigadier to return to billets at 2 a.m.	
	11/3/16		Lt. HARRIS reported for duty and was posted to B Coy. Battalion provided working parties for R.E. A very successful concert was arranged by Capt. FAWKES.	
	12/3/16		Battalion provided working parties. Lt. McINTYRE and BROWN and 2nd Lt. S. BROWN from TYNESIDE SCOTTISH reported for duty and were posted to "A" & "C" Coys. respectively.	

WAR DIARY
INTELLIGENCE SUMMARY

Army Form C. 2118

Place	Date	Hour	Summary of Events and Information	Remarks and references to Appendices
FG-2	13/3/16		Battalion relieved 16 LANCASHIRE FUSILIERS in FG-2 sector. Relief commenced 7.45 p.m. and was satisfactorily completed by 9.30 p.m. Desultory artillery shelling by both sides all day. Also occasional T.M. fire. Prompt and distinctly heard all the rifle and reserve volume were fired into AUTHUILLE by the enemy. Very little reply to M.G. fire.	
	14/3/16		Weather was exceedingly fine and warm. 2nd Lt. ARNAUD reported for duty yesterday from R.F.C. 2nd Lt. GREEN reported from 4th Army School FLIXECOURT. Artillery fairly active on both sides all day. Enemy ? M.G. fire in the afternoon. We retaliated with our T.M.B. and did considerably sniping. Tympanum was heard in THIEPVAL about 7.30 am and was fired upon. Lt. REED reported sick and was evacuated. Weather again fine.	
	15/3/16		Desultory artillery fire by both sides all day with occasional T.M. fire. One shell struck D Coy Headquarters killing one man and wounding three men.	

WAR DIARY or INTELLIGENCE SUMMARY

Army Form C. 2118

Place	Date	Hour	Summary of Events and Information	Remarks and references to Appendices
	16/3/16		Artillery again fired on trenches in THIEPVAL. The trenches have been greatly improved and we are in the fine weather greatly assisting us. A lot of wire has also been erected along our front. Lt. T. BROHN was evacuated with Shell Shock. Everything normal.	
AUTHUILLE	17/3/16		Battalion was relieved by 2nd INNIS. FUS. Relief commenced 8 p.m. was satisfactorily completed by 9.30 p.m. On relief Battalion Coy by Coy proceeded to Billets in AVELUY.	
	18/3/16		Battalion provided working parties for R.E. I visited stages on the village of CONTALMAISON and trenches in front of G.1 and G.2.	
	19/3/16		Batts. also provided working parties. do	
	20/3/16		Battalion relieved 2nd INNIS. FUS. in F.G.2 Subsects. Relief commenced 7 p.m. and was satisfactorily completed by 8.45 p.m.	

WAR DIARY or INTELLIGENCE SUMMARY

Army Form C. 2118

Place	Date	Hour	Summary of Events and Information	Remarks and references to Appendices
F.L. 2	20/3/16		During the night patrols went out from all companies. Enemy sent up a few Verey lights. Day.	
	21/3/16		Enemy sent over the Weldums in direction of Bn. H.Q. Our artillery replied with shrapnel—some. At 5 p.m. our artillery cut away wire in front of 14 & 8. Night fine.	
	22/3/16		Lt. Col. H. H. RITSON V.D. returned to duty from sick leave. Quiet day. During night bombardment heard N. Searchlights seen behind THIEPVAL.	
	23/3/16		Enemy threw many canisters on R31 a 1/1 & R31 a 2/4 5 and Bn M.D. Bombers retaled and fired up near THIEPVAL on THIEPVAL–POZIERES road. At 9.30 pm 10 minutes heavy barrage on R31 c 3/50. The remainder of the night M.A. quiet.	
	24/3/16		Day m.a. quiet in account of wet. Relieved by 2nd INNIS. FUS. Relief complete at 8.55 pm. Battalion returned billets in BOUZINCOURT.	
BOUZINCOURT	25/3/16		Battalion paraded north by parties.	

WAR DIARY
INTELLIGENCE SUMMARY

Army Form C. 2118

Place	Date	Hour	Summary of Events and Information	Remarks and references to Appendices
	26/11/16 27/11/16		Battalion provided working parties.	
	28/3/16		do.	
	29/3/16 30/3/16		Battalion relieved 16th Bn LANCASHIRE FUS. in F.G.1. Relief commenced at 8 p.m. and was satisfactorily completed by 10.30 p.m. Everything very quiet. Trenches in fairly good condition. M.G. fairly active but with the exception of this very little sign of life shown by either side. A good deal of work was needed in front of sectors B & C right of trenches. Everything is drying up fast with the warm weather. Our artillery opened with T.M. Stokes R&Lc & X.1a. from 4 to 4.30 p.m. Enemy retaliation was very quick and continued for about 15 minutes after we finished firing. Very little damage was done to our line. The damage done to enemy trenches was difficult to estimate but a fire occurred, bursts of M.G. fire but very little rifle fire.	
	3/3/16		Trenches in very good condition.	

J. L. Fisher
Major 16th Northd Fus.
Commdg. 16th Northd Fus.

96th Brigade
32nd Division.

16th BATTALION

NORTHUMBERLAND FUSILIERS

APRIL 1 9 1 6;

16th Bn. NORTH'D FUSILIERS.

WAR DIARY or INTELLIGENCE SUMMARY

Place	Date	Hour	Summary of Events and Information	Remarks and references to Appendices
F.9.2 Authuille	1/4/16		The right 1/2 of the subsector from QUARRY, PRAE STREET & MERSEY STREET was taken over by the 11th SHERWOOD FORESTERS. The dividing line of the sector is now MERSEY ST. - CRUCIFIX CORNER. The dispositions of the Coys are now "C" Coy MERSEY STREET - LIME ST. "A" Coy. LIME ST - CHURRENT ST. "B" Coy in support. "D" Coy in dugouts CRUCIFIX CORNER. Everything very quiet.	
	2/4/16		Very occasional artillery fire. M.G. & rifle fire very quiet. Wiring party went out in front of X.1.6. A good deal of wire has been put down during this tour. Nothing much is now more formidable and it was a pleasure to see it taking form. Very fine & warm. Wind S.S.W.	
	3/4/16		Everything fairly quiet until about 8 p.m. when the enemy sent over several rifle grenades in the direction of ROCK ST. No damage done. The Battalion was relieved by the 19th LANCASHIRE FUS. Relief commenced at 7.30 p.m. & was satisfactorily completed by 9.30 p.m. On relief the Battalion proceeded to BOUZINCOURT where it billeted for the night.	

Army Form C. 2118

WAR DIARY
or
INTELLIGENCE SUMMARY
(Erase heading not required.)

Instructions regarding War Diaries and Intelligence Summaries are contained in F. S. Regs., Part II. and the Staff Manual respectively. Title Pages will be prepared in manuscript.

Place	Date	Hour	Summary of Events and Information	Remarks and references to Appendices
BOUZINCOURT	4/4/16		Battalion moved off at 10 a.m. and marched to PIERREGOT arriving there at 4:30 p.m. Men were all given very good billets and should be very comfortable during their rest.	
PIERREGOT	5/4/16		Day spent in cleaning equipment etc. and refitting.	
	6/4/16		Coy training including Bayonet fighting, miring, rapid loading etc.	
	7/4/16		Battalion route march.	
	8/4/16		Coy training.	
	9/4/16		Church Parade.	
	10/4/16		Battalion practised ceremonial drill for G.O.C's inspection on 12/4/16.	
	11/4/16		Coy training.	
	12/4/16		G.O.C. inspected the Bn. on the Corps training ground in review order and then watched the march past. He also inspected the Lewis Gunners at work. The inspection was marred by the rain which poured down steadily all day.	
	13/4/16		Coy training.	
	14/4/16		Battalion route march.	

1875 Wt. W593/826 1,000,000 4/15 J.B.C. & A. A.D.S.S./Forms/C. 2118.

Army Form C. 2118

WAR DIARY
or
INTELLIGENCE SUMMARY
(Erase heading not required.)

Instructions regarding War Diaries and Intelligence Summaries are contained in F. S. Regs., Part II. and the Staff Manual respectively. Title Pages will be prepared in manuscript.

Place	Date	Hour	Summary of Events and Information	Remarks and references to Appendices
	15/4/16		Coy training.	
	16/4/16		Brigade Cross country run in the afternoon. The INNISKILLING FUSILIERS took the first three places. The Battalion coming in fourth. Church Parade.	
	17/4/16		Coy training. Brigade Staff Ride. Commdg. Officers and O.C. Coys attended.	
	18/4/16		Coy training. Brigade Staff Ride. 2nd in Command, Platoon Commanders, Lewis Gun Officer, Bombing Officers and 2 Messengers attended. Ground was unsuitable by the rain.	
	19/4/16		Coy training.	
	20/4/16		do.	
	21/4/16		Battalion Route March.	
	22/4/16		Coy training and preparing to move the following day. The men are very fit after their rest and have thoroughly enjoyed themselves in spite of the inclement weather.	

Army Form C. 2118

WAR DIARY
~~INTELLIGENCE SUMMARY~~
(Erase heading not required.)

Instructions regarding War Diaries and Intelligence Summaries are contained in F.S. Regs., Part II. and the Staff Manual respectively. Title Pages will be prepared in manuscript.

Place	Date	Hour	Summary of Events and Information	Remarks and references to Appendices
	23/4/16		St. George's Day. The Battalion marched from PIERREGOT to SENLIS all ranks wearing red & white roses. The drums were decorated as was also its transport and the Battalion created quite an impression in the villages we passed through. The Battalion billeted in SENLIS for the night. We had as guests to our St. George's Dinner, Brig. General C. YATMAN, Major STEPHENSON. 19th NORTH'D FUS., Capt. A.A. JOHNSON and Capt. T. HARVEY.	
SENLIS	24/4/16		Battalion relieved the 2nd Bn. K.O.Y.L.I. in AUTHUILLE at 11 P.M. "C" Coy garrisoned the KEEPS, 2 Platoons A Coy at CRUCIFIX CORNER, remainder of the Bn. in dugouts at BLACK HORSE RIDGE.	
AUTHUILLE	25/4/16		Battalion provided working parties for R.E.	
	26/4/16		do.	
	27/4/16		do.	
	28/4/16		Battalion relieved 2nd Bn. INNISKILLING FUSILIERS in AUTHUILLE subsects. Relief commenced 10 P.M. and was satisfactorily completed by 11.30 P.M. Everything very quiet.	

WAR DIARY or INTELLIGENCE SUMMARY

Army Form C. 2118

Place	Date	Hour	Summary of Events and Information	Remarks and references to Appendices
AUTHUILLE Sector	29/4/16		Everything fairly quiet during the day. About midnight there was only desultory firing to the North, and at 2.20 am the enemy commenced to bombard our line between W.6.1 and R 31.2. He fixing was very heavy and a barrage was thrown up in CAMPBELL avenue and ISLAY Street. Our artillery retaliated and threw up a barrage in front of enemy frontline. No attempt was made at a raid. Our damage was done to the wire and front line Trenches R31.1 and 2 but there were no casualties.	
	30/4/16		Very little activity on either side. Day spent in repairing damage caused by bombardment. A party under Lt. R.F. moved forward the mine in front of W.6.1 where it is proposed to dig but found. 2nd Lt. M.G. KLEAN noted from the Cadet School reported for duty and was posted to "C" Coy.	

W.E. Robinson
Lt. Col.
Commdg. 16th Bn. Northd Fus.

96th Brigade.

32nd Division.

16th BATTALION

NORTHUMBERLAND FUSILIERS

M A Y 1 9 1 6;

"A" Form.
Army Form C. 2121.

MESSAGES AND SIGNALS.

No. of Message _____

Prefix	Code	Words	Charge	This message is on a/c of:	Recd. at _____ m.
Office of Origin and Service Instructions.		Sent			Date _____
		At _____ m.		_____ Service.	From _____
		To			By _____
		By		(Signature of "Franking Officer.")	

TO: D.A.G 3rd Echelon

| Sender's Number. | Day of Month | In reply to Number | AAA |
| VE227 | 4 | | |

Herewith War Diary for the month of May aaa

From 16 N.F.

Place

Time

The above may be forwarded as now corrected. (Z)

Arthur W. Little

Major

Censor. Signature of Addresser or person authorised to telegraph in his name.
* This line should be erased if not required.

16th Bn. North'd Fus.

16 Northumberland Vol 6

Army Form C. 2118

WAR DIARY
or
INTELLIGENCE SUMMARY
(Erase heading not required.)

Place	Date	Hour	Summary of Events and Information	Remarks and references to Appendices
AUTHUILLE Sector.	1/5/16		Occasional artillery fire by both sides otherwise very quiet. New trench in front of N.6.1 (from OBAN AV. to CHONDENT Cy) was commenced at 10 p.m. The INNIS. FUS. provided the digging parties and worked until 2.15 a.m. by which time they had reached an average depth of 3'. There was no casualty from wounds appeared to be a close shave.	
	2/5/16		The enemy bombarded the sector at frequent intervals during the day with T.H.E. whizzbangs and T.M's. Not a great deal of damage was done to its trenches but a party of our cyclists were wounded, the front line suffered heavily. Our artillery and trench mortars retaliated. The Battalion was relieved by the 2nd INNIS FUS. Relief commenced at 10 p.m. and was completed at 11.15 p.m. H.Q., A & B Coys. proceeding to AVELUY, C & D Coys to CRUCIFIX CORNER.	
AVELUY.	3/5/16		Battalion provided working parties for R.E.	
	4/5/16		do.	
	5/5/16		do.	
			The 15th Bn. LANCS. FUS raided enemy trenches opposite X13 and took	

WAR DIARY
~~INTELLIGENCE SUMMARY~~

(Erase heading not required.)

Army Form C. 2118

Place	Date	Hour	Summary of Events and Information	Remarks and references to Appendices
	6/5/16		five prisoners, four of which were handed over to us & one to L.Dur.H.Q. They were conducted to SENLIS by C. PORTER. The enemy retaliated on our trenches and also on AVELUY but no damage was done in the village although there were several casualties in the trenches. Battalion provided working parties for R.E.	
	7/5/16		Battalion was relieved at 11 p.m. by the 2nd Bn. MANCHESTER REGT. and proceeded into Billets at BOUZINCOURT. C Coy remained in AVELUY to provide working parties at CRUCIFIX CORNER.	
	8/5/16		Battalion provided working parties for R.E. do.	
	9/5/16		Tactical Exercise in skeleton formation was carried out over the ground between BOUZINCOURT WOOD and BAIZIEUX. The C.O., Coy commanders, one N.C.O. per Platoon and messengers attended. The C.O. collapsed when on the tactical scheme and was sent to hospital at WARLOY.	
	10/5/16		Bn provided working parties for R.E. do.	

WAR DIARY or INTELLIGENCE SUMMARY

Army Form C. 2118

Place	Date	Hour	Summary of Events and Information	Remarks and references to Appendices
	11/5/16		Battalion provided working parties.	
	12/5/16		The tactical Exercise practiced on the 9th was repeated. Battalion found working parties for R.E.	
	13/5/16		Battalion was relieved at noon by 2nd INNIS Fus and proceeded into Billets at WARLOY.	
WARLOY	14/5/16		Battalion provided working parties.	
	15/5/16		do.	
	16/5/16		do.	
	17/5/16		Tactical Exercise was carried out by Battalion signallers were found between CONTAY and TOUTENCOURT. The C.O. and the Adjutant were taken up in aeroplanes to watch the exercise. Battalion provided during the afternoon into tents at CONTAY Wood.	
CONTAY WOOD.	18/5/16		Battalion provided working parties. do.	
	19/5/16		At 6.p.m. the Bn. proceeded to BAVLINCOURT Training area and bivouacked until 2 a.m. when an exercise was carried out. Troops returning to Camp about 6.30 a.m.	

Army Form C. 2118

WAR DIARY
or
INTELLIGENCE SUMMARY
(Erase heading not required.)

Place	Date	Hour	Summary of Events and Information	Remarks and references to Appendices
	20/5/16		Battalion provided working parties.	
	21/5/16		Brigade Church Parade at CONTAY and inspection by Brig-Genl YATMAN.	
	22/5/16		Battalion provided working parties. Men on afternoon parties paraded under R.S.M. in the morning & those on morning parties in the afternoon.	
	23/5/16		Do.	
	24/5/16		Battalion men inoculated against paratyphoid.	
	25/5/16		Resting.	
	26/5/16		Battalion still resting after effects of inoculation. All the men that were first inoculated & T.29 & 6 watched demonstration of use of French wire in trenches, French trench mortars firing and employing of trenches. Scheme was not much of a success as T.M. did not appear to be able to get the range.	
	27/5/16		Battalion provided working parties.	
	28/5/16		Brigade Church Parade at CONTAY after which the G.O.C. Division presented ribbons to the officers and N.C.O.'s of 15th LANCS FUS for their work on the night of cutting wire expedition.	

Army Form C. 2118

5.

WAR DIARY
or
INTELLIGENCE SUMMARY
(Erase heading not required.)

Instructions regarding War Diaries and Intelligence Summaries are contained in F.S. Regs., Part II. and the Staff Manual respectively. Title Pages will be prepared in manuscript.

Place	Date	Hour	Summary of Events and Information	Remarks and references to Appendices
AVELUY WOOD.	29/5/16		Battalion moved out from CONTAY WOOD at 6 a.m. and proceeded to BOUZINCOURT arriving there at 9 a.m. It rested was continued at 5.30 p.m. to AVELUY WOOD where the Battalion went under canvas for the night.	
	30/5/16		Battalion relieved 2nd K.O.Y.L.I. in THIEPVAL Subsector at 9 p.m. relief being completed at 11.30 p.m. Night very quiet. Disposition of Coys from right & left A.B.C.D.	
THIEPVAL Subsector.	31/5/16		Desultory shelling and T.M. fire all day but very little damage done. We retaliated with artillery and T.M. N.C.O's fairly quiet except for M.G. fire. Wire had out and a patrol reconnoitred DIAMOND WOOD but did not discover any activity on the part of the enemy.	

Arthur W. Little
Commanding 16th Northd Fus.

B   96th Brigade.
            32nd Division.

1/16th BATTALION

NORTHUMBERLAND FUSILIERS

JUNE 1916:

Army Form C. 2118

1 Bn NORTHD FUSILIERS · XXXII · WAR DIARY or INTELLIGENCE SUMMARY
(Erase heading not required.)

Jun 16 Nollamb Vol 7

Instructions regarding War Diaries and Intelligence Summaries are contained in F.S. Regs, Part II. and the Staff Manual respectively. Title Pages will be prepared in manuscript.

Place	Date	Hour	Summary of Events and Information	Remarks and references to Appendices
THIEPVAL Wood sector.	1/6/16		Enemy artillery + T.M. fairly active during the afternoon & again at night. M.G. was also active during night. Heavy punishment in front of whole sector.	
	2/6/16		Very quiet during the day. T.M. + enemy artillery were again active on two hour turns during the night, but very little damage done. Trenches are in fairly good state of repair.	
	3/6/16		Everything quiet. Battn was relieved by 2nd R.Innis.Fus. and from and proceeded to dugouts at BLACK HORSE BRIDGE. "D" Coy garrisoned the KEEPS.	
BLACK HORSE BRIDGE.	4/6/16		Battalion supplied working parties for THIEPVAL Wood sector. Mail received that Colonel J.W.M. RITSON had lead the C.M.G. conferred upon him, and Sgt H.S. BARNES, "B" Coy, the D.C.M.	
	5/6/16		Battalion supplied working parties for THIEPVAL Wood sector. 11th BORDER Regt raided enemy lines opposite TINDRUM S in AUTHUILLE Wood sector and took 11 prisoners who were taken over to us and sent on to SENLIS. Very few shells fell near BLACK HORSE BRIDGE during the bombardment over	

Army Form C. 2118

WAR DIARY
or
INTELLIGENCE SUMMARY
(Erase heading not required.)

2.

Place	Date	Hour	Summary of Events and Information	Remarks and references to Appendices
	7/6/16		Battalion mounted working parties in the THIEPVAL Intersector. C & D Coys relieved the left and left centre Coys of the 2nd R. INNIS. FUS. at 12 noon in the THIEPVAL Intersector. A & B relieved the right centre and right Coys at 2 am. 9 M.G. supplied 5 dy vr truck from THIEPVAL Pt. NORTH — DIAMOND WOOD — R.25.C.2 and wire was erected last evening M.G. fire prevented the digging party from working.	
THIEPVAL Intersector	8/6/16		Artillery & T.M. of all calibres extremely active throughout the 24 hours. Our trenches were severely damaged. Their dugouts were blown in but the men were without exception unimpaired. Greater activity of artillery & T.M. than on previous day. Two enemy aeroplanes flew over THIEPVAL WOOD. It would have been heavily shelled during the day. Night was quiet. M.G. fire was intermittent.	
	10/6/16		Enemy artillery exceptionally active throughout the day. A & 11.20 pm heavy bombardment of R.I.R. on our left & our our two left Coys.	

Army Form C. 2118

WAR DIARY
or
INTELLIGENCE SUMMARY
(Erase heading not required.)

Instructions regarding War Diaries and Intelligence Summaries are contained in F. S. Regs., Part II and the Staff Manual respectively. Title Pages will be prepared in manuscript.

Place	Date	Hour	Summary of Events and Information	Remarks and references to Appendices
	11/6/16		Reconnoitring shells were used but no raid was attempted on our front.	
	12/6/16		Quiet day, no artillery activity.	
	13/6/16		do	
			Artillery on both sides again quiet. Bn. was relieved by 15th R.W. M.L.I. at 11.30 P.M. and marched into billets at WARLOY-BAILLON arriving there at 4 A.M. 14/6/16. Battalion rested.	
WARLOY	14/6/16			
	15/6/16		Corps lectured barriers in the BAIZIEUX having been acting as Corps Commander addressed all Officers.	
		12.30 P.M.		
	16/4/16		Bn. practised wearing trenches at MEDAVILLE	
	17/6/16		Bn. marched under Coy arrangements.	
	18/6/16		Church Parade after which Maj. Genl. RYCROFT presented D.C.M. to Sgt. H.S. BARNES.	

WAR DIARY
or
INTELLIGENCE SUMMARY

(Erase heading not required.)

Army Form C. 2118

Place	Date	Hour	Summary of Events and Information	Remarks and references to Appendices
	19/6/16		Corps tactical exercise - the BAIZIEUX training area. The Army & Corps Commanders were present and addressed the Officers on completion of the exercise.	
	20/6/16		Practiced morning bugles at P.33 M of 5 I.D.	
	21/6/16		Tactical exercise in BAIZIEUX training Area.	
	22/6/16		Battalion paraded under coy arrangements.	
	23/6/16		Coy practiced tactical exercises in BAIZIEUX training Area.	
	24/6/16		Coy paraded under coy arrangements.	
	25/6/16		Coy paraded for Church Parade in the football field at 9 am.	
	26/6/16		Coy paraded dressed for the attack and were inspected by Major ARCHER. The men looked exceedingly fit & smart. Capt. DUNGLINSON and 2nd G. THORNEYCROFT were wounded and 2nd Lts. G.M. POPPLE and E.F.O. WICKHAM were killed on leaving the trenches after the an instructional tour. Lt. F.A. GEORGE was struck off the strength as from 24/6/16 having transferred to R.F.C.	

Army Form C. 2118.

WAR DIARY
or
INTELLIGENCE SUMMARY
(Erase heading not required.)

Instructions regarding War Diaries and Intelligence Summaries are contained in F.S. Regs., Part II. and the Staff Manual respectively. Title Pages will be prepared in manuscript.

Place	Date	Hour	Summary of Events and Information	Remarks and references to Appendices
	27/4/16		Bn. paraded under Coy arrangements.	
	28/4/16		Bn. went to KNIGHTS REDOUBT, V23, at 9.30 p.m. and bivouacked. Received orders to stand fast, attack postponed for 48 hours.	
	29/4/16		Bn. rested.	
	30/4/16		Bn. moved HQ by Platoons from V23 at 1 P.M. and proceeded to trenches via M.7.1/0 – NORTH AV – MARTINSART – AVELUY ROAD – PIONEER ROAD – AVELUY – HAMEL ROADS – BLACK HORSE BRIDGE, and relieved the 2. R.I.F. in the line from MAISON GRISE SAP exclusive to SKINNER ST. inclusive. Bn. H.Q. was established in GEMMEL ST. A Coy took over the line from SKINNER ST & HAMILTON AV. B Coy took over the line from HAMILTON AV. & MAISON GRISE SAP. C Coy 9.10 Platoons in HAMILTON AV., 11 Platoon in GOURICK ST. 12 Platoon in GREENOCK AV. D Coy in GEMMEL ST. Reliefs were completed by 2.30 a.m. 1st July 1916. W. M. Rutherford Lt. Col. Commdg. 16th N'thd Fus.	

96th Inf.Bde.
32nd Div.

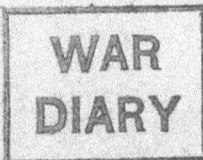

16th BATTN. THE NORTHUMBERLAND FUSILIERS.

J U L Y

1 9 1 6

5.

Army Form C. 2118.

WAR DIARY
or
INTELLIGENCE SUMMARY
(Erase heading not required.)

July

Vol 8

CONFIDENTIAL
WAR DIARY
16th Northumberland Fusiliers

1st July 1916 — 31st July 1916

16. North'd Fus.

Army Form C. 2118

WAR DIARY or INTELLIGENCE SUMMARY
(Erase heading not required.)

Place	Date	Hour	Summary of Events and Information	Remarks and references to Appendices
THIEPVAL SECTOR	1.7.16		Zero hour was fixed for 7.30 am. and at -4- A & B Coys moved forward to about 100x behind our barrage. C Coy moving into the front line trench. When the barrage lifted A & B Coys moved forward in waves & were instantly fired upon by Enemy's M.G. & rifles. The Enemy Coys upon their parapet & opened to our men to come on - picked them off with rifle fire. The Enemy's fire was so intense that the advance was checked the waves at what was left of them, were forced to lie down. On observing this, C Coy the support Coy, moved out to reinforce the front line, being a great number of men. by winning Co. direction of Bn. H.Q. was moved to the front line trench about 50' S. of Hamilton Av. at 7.40 am. & on seeing the position orders were given for D. Coy the reserve Coy to advance. Peering over the parapet they found platoon had a great number of men & the remainder of the Coy was ordered to "stand fast" - held the line.
At 6 am. Brigade H.Q. was advised of the situation & at 10.43 am. orders were received that no last to hang on where we were as they were trying to turn the N. of THIEPVAL. 16th LANCASHIRE FUSILIERS to reinforce us At F.20 am. We asked the 16th to send up two companies. One Coy. looking in the front line trench from MAISON GRISE Coy to HAMILTON AV. the other Coy. remaining a line from GEMMEL ST. arriving there about 10 am
At 9.30 am a message was received from O.C. 96th Bde STOKES	

1875 Wt. W593/826 1,000,000 4/15 J.B.C. & A. A.D.S.S./Forms/C. 2118.

WAR DIARY
or
INTELLIGENCE SUMMARY

(Erase heading not required.)

Army Form C. 2118

Place	Date	Hour	Summary of Events and Information	Remarks and references to Appendices
"BLUFF"	1.7.16 (Contd)		MORTAR Battery, whose gun had been unable to fire from 6.15 am. owing to lack of ammunition, that a fresh supply had arrived. He was ordered to continue firing on the enemy front line in conjunction with our artillery. The enemy's artillery continued firing on "No man's land" & our front line trench all day which no doubt accounted for a large number of the casualties amongst the Coys that went lying out. Our artillery continued to fire all day but it was only very occasionally that it appeared to be heavy & effective. The enemy M.G. fires whenever a movement was shown in the line. Bn. H.Q. moved over to GEMMEL G at 5 P.m. Orders were received from Bde. H.Q. at 9.10 p.m. to withdraw the men who were lying out as it was dark & that we would be relieved by the 16 R.I.F. & 2 R.I.F. after which the Bn. would proceed to the BLUFF. The relief was completed at 11pm and the remnants of the Bn. 6 Officers & 279 O.R. marched into the BLUFF at about 1.30 a.m. A Coy of the 2. R.I.F. commanded by Capt. WILLIAMS rendered excellent work in carrying keen the wounded men who were lying out. Our L.O. also did good work all day as did everybody who took part in the attack. The men of the attacking Coys moved forward to the man until the murderous fire of the enemy's M.G. forced them to halt. Not a man moved — after nightfall we found in several places straight lines of ten or twelve dead or badly wounded not a step (platoons had not been checked for yards.	

Army Form C. 2118

WAR DIARY
or
INTELLIGENCE SUMMARY

(Erase heading not required.)

Instructions regarding War Diaries and Intelligence Summaries are contained in F. S. Regs., Part II and the Staff Manual respectively. Title Pages will be prepared in manuscript.

Place	Date	Hour	Summary of Events and Information	Remarks and references to Appendices
AVELUY WOOD	2.7.16		The Bn rested all day at the BLUFF & at night moved to "C" Assembly Trenches in AVELUY WOOD.	
	3.7.16		The Bn did no work except to attend to their Arms & Equipment. A roll call was held at which 6 Officers 205 O.R. answered their names, which made the Casualties, killed, wounded missing, 13 Officers & 365 O.R. The Bn moved at 6.30 pm to WARLOY via BOUZINCOURT & route, arriving there about 9 p.m.	
WARLOY	4.7.16		Day spent in clearing up & the re-organisation of the Bn. was commenced	
	5.7.16		The Bn. marched at 5 pm to LEALVILLERS via VARENNES arriving there about 7 p.m.	
LEALVILLERS	6.7.16		Bn. paraded under Coy. arrangements - practised Bayonet fighting, Physical training etc. A. H.Q. Coy was formed of all details in the Bn.	
	7.7.16		The Bn. moved at 3.30 p.m. to HEADAUVILLE via VARENNES arriving here about 4.30 p.m. At 6.30 p.m. the Bn. moved to Bn. paraded under Coy. arrangements.	
	8.7.16		SENLIS arriving there about 9 p.m. Church Parade at 11 a.m.	
SENLIS	9.7.16		The Bn. moved at 4 p.m. to BOUZINCOURT & was bivouaced in a field at BOUZINCOURT. W.T.C. 50. Surplus Officers - specialists were left behind with the Transport. Kits noted to bivouc on the road between SENLIS and BOUZINCOURT.	

WAR DIARY
or
INTELLIGENCE SUMMARY

Army Form C. 2118

(Erase heading not required.)

Place	Date	Hour	Summary of Events and Information	Remarks and references to Appendices
	10.7.16		Bn. paraded under Coy arrangements for Bayonet fighting, Physical Training &c.	
	11.7.16		Bn. paraded under Coy arrangements. Bn. moved off at 11.30 p.m. & proceeded to OUILLERS. Route was branched from the 2nd MANCHESTER REGT. Charge of the Battalion was 315 O.R. Our artillery was very active all night with very little retaliation from the Enemy.	
OUILLERS	12.7.16		Continued activity on both sides.	
	13.7.16		One platoon of A Coy was early in the morning to support the 19th LANCASHIRE FUSILIERS — helped to repulse a counter attack.	
	14.7.16		Attempt was made to advance to — consolidate Pts 45 and 63, but we were held up by M.G. & strong bombing parties 1/7 H.L.I. & 2nd R.I.F. who passed thro' our right were driven back to their original line which they held repulsing the counter-attack. Bn. was relieved at 7.30 p.m. by 2nd MANCHESTER REGT. & proceeded to BOUZINCOURT — billeted for the night.	
BOUZINCOURT	15.7.16		Battalion moved to WARLOY. G.O.C. 32nd Division inspected us on the march & expressed his satisfaction at the smartness of the men & congratulated us on the work we had done.	
WARLOY	16.7.16		Battalion proceeded to BEAUVAL via VARENNES, LEALVILLERS, ARQUEVES — RAINCHEVAL — BEAUQUESNE — Road junction G.30 a 10.10 — road junction G.16 D 70.60 and went into billets. The following Officers reported for duty. Capt N. SMITH from 15th K AND N'TH'D FUS. 2nd Lt. E. W. PYLE, 2nd Lt. Q. E. PIERREPOINT, 2nd Lt. W. M. RUTHERFORD, 2nd Lt. L. STEEDMAN, 2nd Lt. N. R. FUTERS, 2nd Lt. TE DAWSON all from 3rd NORTH'D.	
BEAUVAL	17.7.16		Battalion moved to NEUVILLETTE via DOULLENS and HTE.VILLE.	

Army Form C. 2118

WAR DIARY
or
INTELLIGENCE SUMMARY
(Erase heading not required.)

Instructions regarding War Diaries and Intelligence Summaries are contained in F.S. Regs., Part II. and the Staff Manual respectively. Title Pages will be prepared in manuscript.

Place	Date	Hour	Summary of Events and Information	Remarks and references to Appendices
NEUVILLETTE	16.7.16		Battalion rested. Coy. inspections took place during the day.	
	19.7.16		Battalion moved to BLANGERVAL.	
BLANGERVAL	20.7.16		Battalion moved to ANVIN via SIRACOURT - CROIX - X roads. 200 yards West of CHAPELLE	
ANVIN	21.7.16		VILLEMETZ - LIBESSART - FLEURY and went into Billets. Bn moved to FONTAINE-LES-HERMANS via FONTAINES-BOUBANS - X roads	
FNTAIN-LES-HERMANS	22.7.16		½ mile S of MONT CORNET and went into Billets. Interior Economy of Companies.	
	23.7.16		Brigade Church Parade at 9 am. Capt FRENCH, C.F. officiating.	
	24.7.16		Coy training + classes continued in Bombing, Lewis Guns etc. The following Officers reported for duty. 2nd Lt E.W. DUNN from 3rd NORTH'D FUS. 2nd Lt R.C. MILLS from 15th NORTH'D FUS. 2nd Lt H.Q. KING from 15th NORTH'D FUS.	
	25.7.16		Coy training.	
	26.7.16		Battalion moved to LABEUVRIERE via FERFAY - CAUCHY a la TOUR - AUCHEL - LOZINGHEM - X road D 25 b. 2.5. then into Billets. Orders received to detail two platoons to report at LA	
LABEUVRIERE	27.7.16		BUISSIERE on the 28th inst at Corps troops. Battalion inspected by the Commanding Officer, after which the men for Corps troops were chosen. Lewis Gun, Signalling, Bombing Courses continued.	
	28.7.16		The 2 platoons detailed as Corps troops under the Command of Lt White with Lt G. Leach as second in Command, proceeded to LA BUISSIERE. Courses continued.	
	29.7.16		Battalion moved to HOUCHIN via Cross roads D 21 a. 6. 7. - LES CHARMEUX - HESDIGNEUL	
HOUCHIN			+ went into Camp to the E side of the village.	
	30.7.16		Courses continued. Church Parade at 11.30 am. Capt FRENCH officiated. Courses continued. 2nd Lt E.F. WHITE wounded on 1st July in the advance on	
	31.7.16		THIEPVAL reported for duty.	

Wm Johnson
O.C. 16 (s) Bn. North'd Fus. Lt Col.

1875 Wt. W593/826 1,000,000 4/15 J.B.C. & A. A.D.S.S./Forms/C. 2118.

96th Brigade.

32nd Division.

16th BATTALION

NORTHUMBERLAND FUSILIERS

AUGUST 1916

Confidential

Vol 9

War Diary
16th North Stand
from 1st August 1916 to 31st August 1916

16" Bn. NORTHD FUS.

Army Form C. 2118

WAR DIARY
or
INTELLIGENCE SUMMARY

(Erase heading not required.)

Instructions regarding War Diaries and Intelligence Summaries are contained in F.S. Regs., Part II. and the Staff Manual respectively. Title Pages will be prepared in manuscript.

Place	Date	Hour	Summary of Events and Information	Remarks and references to Appendices
HOUCHIN	1.6.16		Specialist Courses continued. Draft of 196 O.R. arrived, made up from 1st, 3rd & 8th, 9th, 12th, 16th, 17th, 18th, 20th, 26th & 31st Bns. Northumberland Fusiliers. Specialist Courses continued. Draft medically examined remainders	
	2.6.16	11 A.M.	Echoed from Eagles. 2.Lt. T.H. MAKE joined Bn. 2.7.16. 2.Lt. H.F. WHITE — do — Recd. 2.7.16. Coy. Kit inspection	
	3.8.16		Bn. route march to LA BUISSIERE.	
	4.6.16		Specialist Courses continued.	
	5.6.16		Specialist courses continued. Battalion moved to BETHUNE. Went into Billets at the Tobacco Factory.	
BETHUNE	6.6.16		Bn. attended Church Parade in commemoration of the 2nd Anniversary of the commencement of the war held in the Grande Place. BETHUNE. Lt. Col. W.N. Ritson. CMG, VD, relinquished command of the Bn, which was taken over by 2nd in Command. Major E. Archer was appointed 2nd in Command.	
	7.6.16		Battalion paraded under Coy. arrangements for Coy training including Bayonet fighting, Smoke Helmet Drill, Tactical Bombing Exercise, Consolidation of Crater forming ground at E.16.d.40.70. There is an excellent crater made by a large calibre shell at E.17.6.50.40. Specialist Courses continued.	
	8.6.16		— do —	
	9.6.16		— do —	
	10.8.16		— do —	
	11.6.16		Bn. was inspected at work by O.a.C. 52nd Division. Maj. Generals Rycroft. Bn. paraded under Coy. arrangements for Coy. training. Specialist Courses continued.	

1875 Wt. W593/326 1,000,000 4/15 J.B.C. & A. A.D.S.S./Forms/C. 2118.

Army Form C. 2118

WAR DIARY
or
INTELLIGENCE SUMMARY
(Erase heading not required.)

Instructions regarding War Diaries and Intelligence Summaries are contained in F.S. Regs., Part II. and the Staff Manual respectively. Title Pages will be prepared in manuscript.

Place	Date	Hour	Summary of Events and Information	Remarks and references to Appendices
BETHUNE	12.6.16		Bn. en-route march to Pt. D. 24 a. 8. 7. Bn. was inspected en route by G.O.C. 96: R. Inf. Bde. Brig. Genl. YATMAN.	
	13.6.16		Church Parade.	
	14.8.16		Bn. paraded under Coy. arrangements for Coy. training. Specialist courses continued under 2nd Lt. R.E.M. FINLAYSON reported for duty from 147? Bde. M.G. Coy.	
	15.8.16		Bn. paraded under Coy. arrangements for Coy. training. Specialist courses continued. At 6.30 p.m. Battalion marched to D. 24. a. 8. 7. + carried out tactical scheme under command of Capt. T.H. WAKE, returning at 6 a.m. 16.6.16. Battalion inspected in F.S.M.O. at 3 p.m. by Brig. Genl. O. YATMAN, G.O.C. 96 R. INF.	
	16.8.16		BDE.	
	17.6.16		Bn. paraded under Coy. arrangements for Coy. training. Specialist courses continued.	
	18.6.16		Bn. paraded for en-route march. Men cooked their own dinners.	
	19.8.16		Bn. paraded under Coy. arrangements for Coy. training. Specialist courses continued. Church Parade.	
	20.6.16		Bn. relieves 2nd. K.O.Y.L.I. in left sub sector of CAMBRIN sector. A.D. on the right B.C. on the right. Relief completed at 4.45 p.m.	
CAMBRIN Left sub sector	21.6.16		Everything fairly quiet during the right.	
	22.6.16		Desultory shelling + T.M. fire all day by both sides. Enemy did very little damage to out trenches. Patrol left trench at 12.15 a.m. at B.7 an 10 trenches did not discover anything of importance.	
	23.6.16		Occasional small bombardments by the enemy with artillery. T.M. also rifle grenades, we retaliated - silenced them each time. About 9 p.m. one of our men was blown on the right of the Bn. on our right. This caused the enemy to send over T.M. rifle grenades about Bayanne 15" 16. the majority HIGH ST. + caused very little damage. Casualties 1 O.R. killed 7. O.R. wounded. 1 O.R. missing.

1875 M. W. 593/826. 1,000,000. 4/15. A.B.C.& A.Ltd. D.S.S./Forms/C.2118/4.

Army Form C. 2118

WAR DIARY
or
INTELLIGENCE SUMMARY
(Erase heading not required.)

Place	Date	Hour	Summary of Events and Information	Remarks and references to Appendices
	24.8.16		Very quiet night. Morning. About 2.30 p.m. the enemy commenced to bombard the cap at Bryans 15" and considerable damage to L.Cav.T.M. Artillery retaliates. Bombardment ceases about an hour. Our artillery bombarded A 27 & 7.6 & 7.9 at 11.40 p.m. Enemy retaliates keenly but did very little damage to the line. Casualties 1 killed & 1 wounded at.	
CAMBRIN VILLAGE LINE	25.8.16		Desultory shelling & T.M. by both sides. 2nd R. INNIS. FUSILIERS relieved Bn. during afternoon, relief being completed by 5 p.m. On relief Bn. withdrew to village lie. ARTHUR & KEEP garrisons by men from A Coy & S.MS KEEP by men from B Coy. Casualties 2nd L & T Arthur & 2 O.R. wounded	
	26.8.16		Bn. provided fatigue parties for Battalion in the line.	
	27.8.16		— do —	
	28.8.16		— do —	
CAMBRIN LEFT SUB SECTOR	29.8.16	5.30 p.m.	Bn. relieved 2nd Bn. R.I.F. in CAMBRIN left Sub sector. Relief was completed disposition of Coys. A Coy on right. B Coy on left.	
			16 LAN. FUS. sent up a party of 2 officers and 30 o.r. to open out trench between Bryans 15 & 16. They commenced work at 1 a.m. & worked until 5.45 a.m. but did not succeed in clearing the whole trench. The weather was very bad, which no doubt, accounts for the slowness of the work. Casualties Nil. Wind S.W.	
	30.8.16		Everything very quiet during the night. At noon enemy fires here & there. Everything being quiet during the morning. Our Artillery retaliates with 2 salvos 9th M. Son between our front line & enemy's front line. Enemy 3 p.m. shells enemy's front line. Great promptitude. Enemy 3 p.m. shells enemy's front line. Retaliation very feeble. Trenches in a very wet & dirty condition with the rain but quickly being put to rights. Casualties Nil. Wind S.W.	
	31.8.16		But enemies very quiet day. Men all hard at work clearing trenches & lines trench is now in a fairly good state. Enemy fired a few shells during the afternoon being but the others way done to our trenches. We retaliated with artillery & T.M.	

Casualties Nil. Wind S.W.

AnLittle T. Col. ?? ?? ?? ??

96th Brigade.

32nd Division.

16th BATTALION

NORTHUMBERLAND FUSILIERS

SEPTEMBER 1 9 1 6

Vol 10

Original

CONFIDENTIAL.

WAR DIARY

of

16th (Service) Battalion, Northumberland Fusiliers.

from 1st September 1916 to 30th September 1916.

(Volume 10)

WAR DIARY or INTELLIGENCE SUMMARY

Army Form C. 2118

Map ref. 36c N.E.

Place	Date	Hour	Summary of Events and Information	Remarks and references to Appendices
	1.9.16		At 5.15 am. Artillery carried out scheme of retaliation for BETHUNE. Enemy retaliated with artillery & T.M. on our trenches & slightly damages BOYAU H. Remainder of day very quiet except for occasional T.M. activity. Casualties NIL.	A.47a
ANNEQUIN	2.9.16		Occasional shelling by the enemy but no damage done. The retaliates with artillery & T.M. Casualties 6 O.R. wounded. 2nd Bn. R.I.F. Battalion was relieved by 2nd Bn. R.I.F. Relief was completed by 12 pm. Bn went into Bde Reserve at ANNEQUIN. Bn. provided working parties for 206th & 218th F. Coy R.E.	F.23d.
	3.9.16		do	
	4.9.16		do	
	5.9.16		do	
CAMBRIN LEFT SUB-SECTION	6.9.16		Bn. relieved 2nd Bn. R.I.F. in CAMBRIN left sub-section. Considerable artillery & T.M. activity between 4 pm & 7 pm. Spring N.E. Casualties NIL. Relief completed 2.30 pm. Very quiet morning & early afternoon. About 3.30 pm. Considerable activity with T.M. & artillery, no damage done. Very quiet night.	A.27L
	7.9.16		Casualties NIL. Wind N.E.	
	8.9.16		At 1.40 am. raiding party 16 L.F. went out from BOYAU 6 but were unable to cut the wire & had to return. Enemy's retaliation to our barrage was very weak & did no damage to our trenches. Enemy very quiet until about 6 p.m. when one a few T.M. we retaliated with T.M. & artillery lately. Casualties 1 O.R. accidentally wounded. Summary of evidence taken on the charge of REDFEARN. This man left the trenches on acting service deserting his Coy. Bryce, against 8/18336 Pte M. REDFEARN at G Pol on the 27th August	
	9.9.16		Everything very quiet afternoon. Early morning & when MFT was apprehended by selwyn at 5.0 when feet actually back at 5.5 where feet actually back ST obeying no orders	

Army Form C. 2118

Musl 36 C N E

WAR DIARY
or
INTELLIGENCE SUMMARY
(Erase heading not required.)

Instructions regarding War Diaries and Intelligence Summaries are contained in F.S. Regs., Part II. and the Staff Manual respectively. Title Pages will be prepared in manuscript.

Place	Date	Hour	Summary of Events and Information	Remarks and references to Appendices
	9.9.16 (contd)		We retaliated with T.M.s + artillery which shut him up. Our T.M.s cut off opposite Bryan 12 from 5.30 p.m. to about 7 p.m. Enemy retaliates with T.M. + shrapnel but did no damage. Casualties NIL. Wind N.E.	
CAMBRIN (VILLAGE LINE)	10.9.16		Bn. relieved by 2. R.I.F. Relief was completed 8.30 a.m. when Bn. withdrew to VILLAGE LINE at Brigade support. Casualties 2 wounded. Wind N.E. Bn. provided carrying parties for T.M. B's + R.E.	A.27.4.
	11.9.16		do — do	
	12.9.16		do — do	
	13.9.16		do — do	
	14.9.16		Bn relieved 2nd R.I.F. in CAMBRIN left subsection. Relief was completed at 4.15 p.m. Everything very quiet. Casualties NIL. Wind N.N.W.	do
CAMBRIN (LEFT SUBSECTION)	15.9.16		Occasional T.M. fire to which our T.M.s retaliated. Everything exceptionally quiet. Casualties NIL.	
	16.9.16		T.M.s on both sides active at 11 a.m, 3 p.m + 6 p.m. No damage done to our trenches. Very little artillery activity. Casualties NIL. Relief by 5th ROYAL SCOTS cancelled.	
	17.9.16		Another very quiet day. Slight T.M. activity during the afternoon. Casualty 1 O.R. wounded.	
BEUVRY	18.9.16		Bn relieved by 5th Bn ROYAL SCOTS + on relief proceeded to billets at BEUVRY. F14.c. A lot of work was done to improve the drainage of the sub section. Channels were cut in each + front line trench - anything which would run.	
	19.9.16		Day spent in cleaning after attainments for Musketry practice. Several	
	20.9.16		Bn paraded with Of attainments for Musketry Practice. Several Officers went to Sheedee Divisional Gas School at BEUVRY.	

1875 Wt. W593/826 1,000,000 4/15 J.B.C. & A. A.D.S.S./Forms/C.2118.

WAR DIARY
or
INTELLIGENCE SUMMARY

(Erase heading not required.)

Army Form C. 2118

Place	Date	Hour	Summary of Events and Information	Remarks and references to Appendices
BEUVRY.	21.9.16		Coys. practiced wiring, bombing & bayonet fighting.	F14c
	22.9.16		Bn. route march.	
	23.9.16		Working Parties.	
	24.9.16		Church Parade. Wiring, bayonet, bombing practices.	
	25.9.16		Working Parties. A team of 25 O.R. under 2. Lieut. to gether with Kemp from the other Battalions in the Brigade gave a demonstration at ANNEZIN	
			of carrying a Crater.	A 20 G
CUINCHY (SUPPORT LINE)	26.9.16		The Bn. relieves the 2nd K.O.Y.L.I. on the CUINCHY, Support Line, taking over the KEEPS. Provided working & carrying Parties for the R.E. T.M.Bs.	
	27.9.16		do — do — do	
	28.9.16		do — do — do	
	29.9.16		Provided carrying Parties for the T.M.Bs.	
CUINCHY (RIGHT SUB-SECTION)	30.9.16		The Bn. relieves the 2nd R.I.F. in the right CUINCHY subsection. Relief was completed at 2.40 p.m. Disposition of Coys. right to left A.D.B. with C. Coy. in support. Considerable T.M. M.G. activity.	A 21 L

Diary
16 North'd. Inf
—
Sept. 1916

96th Brigade.

32nd Division.

16th BATTALION

NORTHUMBERLAND FUSILIERS.

OCTOBER 1 9 1 6

Army Form C. 2118

Vol II

WAR DIARY
INTELLIGENCE SUMMARY
(Erase heading not required.)

1/6(5) Bn. Northumberland Fusiliers.

War Diary.

Period 1-31st October 1916.

Volume II.

WAR DIARY
or
INTELLIGENCE SUMMARY
(Erase heading not required.)

Army Form C. 2118

Place	Date	Hour	Summary of Events and Information	Remarks and references to Appendices
CUINCHY RIGHT SUB-SECTION	1.10.16		Slight T.M. activity. Artillery quiet. Fairly quiet during the night. Casualties 1 OR wounded.	Maps of 36 B N.E.
	2.10.16		Slight artillery fire but slight T.M. activity. Midnight 2/9 Kerain in the artillery fire F.144pm. At 9.33pm, 10.29pm F.144pm, T.M., M.E., L.G., rifles co-operated with 6" Div. in a T.M. Bombardment. Our trenches considerably damaged by T.M. retaliation with 6" Div.	
	3.10.16		Another quiet day. Nothing of any note occurred until co-operation with 6" Div. at the same hour as the previous night, when our trenches were again damaged by T.M. fire. Same men in GIBSON Sap but impossible to identify regiment.	
LE QUESNOY	4.10.16		Morning very quiet. Battalion relieved by 2nd Bn. R.I.F. & withdrew to Billets at LE QUESNOY in Brigade Reserve.	
	5.10.16		Bn. furnished working parties for the line	
	6.10.16		do	
	7.10.16		do	
CUINCHY RIGHT SUB-SECTION	8.10.16		Bn. relieved 2nd R.I.F. in CUINCHY right sub-section. Relief completed 11.30am. One T.M. activity. Gunnery reported no enemy activity.	
	9.10.16		Bn. was relieved by 10th E. Surrey Regt & 2nd K.O.Y.L.I. + on relief proceeded to BETHUNE.	
	10.10.16			
BETHUNE	11.10.16		Company training. Shortages of equipment partially made up.	
	12.10.16		Battalion Route march.	
	13.10.16		Draft of 249 O.R. arrived to reinforce the Battalion. Fallynia in BETHUNE were inspected by the Battalion.	
	14.10.16		G.O.C. Brigade (96th Bde.) inspected draft. Bayonet fighting under Corps instructions. Route march.	
DIEVAL	15.10.16		Bn. paraded in full marching order & proceeded to DIEVAL. Draft of 14 men arrived.	

Army Form C. 2118

WAR DIARY
or
INTELLIGENCE SUMMARY
(Erase heading not required.)

Instructions regarding War Diaries and Intelligence Summaries are contained in F. S. Regs., Part II. and the Staff Manual respectively. Title Pages will be prepared in manuscript.

Place	Date	Hour	Summary of Events and Information	Remarks and references to Appendices
FREVILLERS	16.10.16		Proceeded to FREVILLERS.	
GOUY-EN-TERNOIS	17.10.16		Continued the march reached GOUY-EN-TERNOIS at 2 pm.	
AMPLIER	18.10.16		Paraded at 6 am marched to AMPLIER where the battalion was in huts.	
TERRAMESNIL	19.10.16		Marched to TERRAMESNIL.	
AMPLIER	20.10.16		Returned to huts at AMPLIER.	
HARPONVILLE	21.10.16		Marched to HARPONVILLE.	
	22.10.16		Remained in billets at HARPONVILLE.	
BRICKFIELDS ALBERT	23.10.16		Proceeded to BRICKFIELDS, ALBERT, S. of VADENCOURT, WARLOY, HENENCOURT, MILLENCOURT, and there went under canvas.	
	24.10.16		Remained in tents owing to very heavy rain. Colonel went to MOUQUET FARM.	
	25.10.16		Rain continued. Officers were taken by Res. Major to neighbourhood of COURCELETTE.	
WARLOY	26.10.16		Battalion returned to WARLOY by way of BOUZINCOURT and SENLIS.	
	27.10.16		Battalion paraded under Coy arrangements for bayonet fighting, bombing and practising the stages of the attack. Training very much affected owing to weather.	
	28.10.16		Carried on with training, weather again very bad.	
	29.10.16		Church Parade. Very heavy rain.	
	30.10.16		Bde. Tactical exercise was intended but had to be cancelled owing to very heavy rain.	
HERISSART	31.10.16		Battalion proceeded to HERISSART via VADENCOURT and CONTAY.	

Arthur W. Tittle Colonel 16 Worcesters

96th Brigade.

32nd Division.

16th BATTALION

NORTHUMBERLAND FUSILIERS

NOVEMBER 1 9 1 6

W A R   D I A R Y.

16th NORTHUMBERLAND FUSILIERS.

From November 1st to 30th. 1916.

VOLUME 12.

WAR DIARY
or
INTELLIGENCE SUMMARY

(Erase heading not required.)

Army Form C. 2118

Instructions regarding War Diaries and Intelligence Summaries are contained in F. S. Regs., Part II. and the Staff Manual respectively. Title Pages will be prepared in manuscript.

Place	Date	Hour	Summary of Events and Information	Remarks and references to Appendices
HERISSART	1-11-16		The Bn. took part in Bde. Tactical Exercise during the morning. In the afternoon Bn. paraded under Coy. arrangements for Coy. training.	
	2-11-16		Heavy rain prevented outdoor training. Lectures were held in billets.	
	3-11-16		The Bn. took part in Bde. Tactical Exercise during the morning and Coy. training afternoon.	
	4-11-16		The Bn. took part in Bde. Tactical Exercise. G.O.C. 32nd Div. witnessed all officers on completion of the scheme. Bn. Enemy Competition took place during the afternoon.	
	5-11-16		Church parade. In the afternoon Bn. paraded for Tactical Scheme.	
	6-11-16		Coy training and lectures during the morning. In the afternoon Bn. paraded for Tactical Scheme.	
	7-11-16		Heavy rain prevented outdoor training. Lectures were held in billets. In the afternoon Bn. went for route march.	
	8-11-16		Rain again prevented outdoor training during the morning and lectures were held. Bn. carried on with Coy training during the afternoon.	
	9-11-16		Bn. took part in Bde. Tactical exercise on the morning. Coy training during the afternoon.	
	10-11-16		Bn. carried out tactical exercise.	
	11-11-16		Bn. took part in tactical exercise. Was present and on the termination of the exercise together with 16th LANCS. FUS. The G.O.C. 32nd Div. the Military Band.	
	12-11-16		Church parade.	
WARLOY	13-11-16		Bn. moved to WARLOY. Bn. carried on with Coy training in the afternoon.	
SCHWABEN REDOUBT	14-11-16		Bn. moved to the line via BOUZINCOURT - AVELUY - CRUCIFIX CORNER where it was met by guides from 16th Bn. RIFLE BRIGADE. Bn relieved remainder of the RIFLE BRIGADE in SCHWABEN REDOUBT. The remainder of the Bn. in support to the enemy old front line. The Bn. was	
	15-11-16		considerable artillery activity on both sides but very little fell on the vicinity of the Bn. was holding.	
	16-11-16		Artillery again active. A few had shells fell in the vicinity of HQ.	
MAILLY MAILLET	17-11-16		Bn. was withdrawn from the line and proceeded to MAILLY MAILLET the 96 Inf. Bde. in reserve to 32nd Div.	

WAR DIARY or INTELLIGENCE SUMMARY

(Erase heading not required.)

Army Form C. 2118

Place	Date	Hour	Summary of Events and Information	Remarks and references to Appendices
MAILLY MAILLET	18-11-16		Bn. at rest Bt.	
ELLIS SQUARE	19-11-16		Bn. attached to 14th Inf Bde and proceeded into reserve at ELLIS SQUARE at 4pm. Bn. on arrival to send two companies A and D to reinforce 1st DORSETS.	57D N.E.
K35c. 45.65 & K35c. 54.82 & K35c. 73.70	20-11-16		C. Coy Bn. relieved the 10th Bn. H.L.I. in the trenches from K.35c.45.65 to K.35c.54.72 & K.35c.73.70. B. Coy in the right Coy on the right. C. Coy in the left. Coy on the left. Bn. H.Q. active. Smoking allowed and permit chocolate was to conduct any fire attack. Employed to establish communication established with K.S.L.I. on our right and 1st DORSETS on our left.	
K35c. 45.65 & K35c. 54.82 & K35c. 73.70 & K35d. 50.60	21-11-16		Artillery again active. Artillery some damage done to our trenches. Employed to improve condition of parapets, as the mud was very sticky and would not hold shape. A and D Coys relieved 1st DORSETS and came on at 7pm. Line now runs from K.35a. 45.65, K.35a. 54.82, K.35c. 73.70 & K.35d. 50.60. Communication established with K.S.L.I. on our right.	57D N.E.
	22-11-16		Desultory artillery fire all day. Condition of trenches not improved.	
	23-11-16		Orders received from 14th Inf Bde to attempt to capture front 88m French mining post up the track towards point 17 (of REDAN street). Two platoons of B Coy were ordered to make a frontal attack on the enemy post. Last platoon of D Coy. A Coy to work up the front of right of Bank of D Coy so as to endeavour and not be employed but actively used on their right. Zero time 5.30. Barrage to be employed but actively used on their right. Zero time 5.30. Barrage of the enemy trenches. On attempt the men going on the vicinity of the enemy trenches. Our artillery were the cause of some of our casualties. The attack failed owing to the heavy condition of the ground. Some of the men stuck in and could not and had to dug out. Men on returning different and dangers back as the enemy fired the trench in front and constantly employed our movements by showers of shooting. Bn. relieved at 5 am by 2nd Bn. GORDONS and proceeded to MAILLY MAILLET.	
RAINECHEVAL	24-11-16		MAILLY MAILLET 1/am and proceeded to RAINECHEVAL and billeted for the night. L.H.C.

WAR DIARY
or
INTELLIGENCE SUMMARY
(Erase heading not required.)

Army Form C. 2118

Place	Date	Hour	Summary of Events and Information	Remarks and references to Appendices
AMPLIER	25-11-16		Bn. proceeded to AMPLIER and billeted for the night	
BONNEVILLE	26-11-16		Bn. proceeded to BONNEVILLE via BEAUVAL - VALHEUREUX and arrived into billets	
	27-11-16		Bn. rested. Men cleaned equipment, arms etc.	
	28-11-16		" " " " "	
	29-11-16		Bn. paraded river by arrangements for section drill, physical training and bayonet fighting. In the afternoon inter company football matches were played.	
	30-11-16		Bn. proceeded to baths at DOMART.	

E.H.L.

A.W.Little Lt.Col.
Commdg 16 North'n Inf.

96th Brigade.

32nd Division.

16th BATTALION

NORTHUMBERLAND FUSILIERS

DECEMBER 1 9 1 6

Vol 77
13

Confidential.

WAR DIARY

of

16th (Service) Bn. Northumberland Fusiliers

from 1st December 1916.   to   31st December 1916.

Vol. 13.

Army Form C. 2118

WAR DIARY
or
INTELLIGENCE SUMMARY
(Erase heading not required.)

Instructions regarding War Diaries and Intelligence Summaries are contained in F.S. Regs., Part II. and the Staff Manual respectively. Title Pages will be prepared in manuscript.

Place	Date	Hour	Summary of Events and Information	Remarks and references to Appendices
BONNEVILLE	1/12/16		Bn. paraded under Coy arrangements for section and platoon drill. Physical training and bayonet fighting. Parties granted to N.C.O.'s of first N on BONNEVILLE. LENS Salle 11 Parts shown a bullet fatigue parties for bombing, bayonet fighting etc.	LENS. Mat 11. Square K.D.
	2/12/16		- do -	
	3/12/16		Church Parades	
	4/12/16		Bn. inspected by G.O.C. 96th Inf Bde. A number of men have failed to get their equipment and obviously cleaned which caused comment by the Brigadier. Bn spent afternoon in stripping and cleaning equipment.	
	5/12/16		Bn. paraded for Bde rehearsal for Battle inspection to be held on 6th Dec 1916. Bombing competition was held in the afternoon.	
	6/12/16		The Bn. of 96th Bde. were inspected by the G.O.C. 5th Corps. Bns were drawn up in close column of Coy's in line with each Coy (from Kamfoints and transport in rear. After being inspected Bns marched past. In the afternoon work was continued on bombing and bayonet fighting troops.	
	7/12/16		Two Coys worked on shaft by training and two Coys worked on trenches. Re-Coy's from 9am to 10am on drill.	
	8/12/16		Remainder of day spent in digging trenches.	
	9/12/16		Bn spent morning digging trenches. Footbll competition were played off during the afternoon. Major R. PERMAIN joined for duty from 96th T.R.C.	
	10/12/16		Church Parade. Draft of 152 men reported for duty	
	11/12/16		Bn route march. Route VALHEUREUX - CANDAS - MEZVILLERS.	
	12/12/16		A Coy carried out musketry. The other Coys paraded for platoon and Coy training. Drill agents	
	13/12/16		Bde route march. BERNEUL - FIENVILLERS - MONTRELET. Coys formed in afternoon	
	14/12/16		A Coy musketry 30yd range. 2 Coys day training. 1 Coy digging bayonet fighting trenches. Draft were training. Time of Coys Coy Coyractice A & B, B & B1	
	15/12/16		B Coy musketry on 30yd range. 3 Coys day training. Draft carried on operate on the trained ground with platoon drill.	
	16/12/16		C Coy musketry on 30yds ranges. A & B physical training and bayonet fighting. B Coy by trng. D Coy digging trenches.	Whole Copy

Army Form C. 2118

WAR DIARY
or
INTELLIGENCE SUMMARY
(Erase heading not required.)

Instructions regarding War Diaries and Intelligence Summaries are contained in F. S. Regs., Part II. and the Staff Manual respectively. Title Pages will be prepared in manuscript.

Place	Date	Hour	Summary of Events and Information	Remarks and references to Appendices
BONNEVILLE	17-12-16 18-12-16		Church Parade. 2nd Lt. Worthington & 2nd Lt. Payton returned for duty. Bn. furnished 500 fatigue to Rest School. Drill. Range. Instructed by Lt. A.B.C.	LENS. 77. 6.D.
	19-12-16		Day musketry on 30 yds range. Draft under instruction. The Bn. was partially fitted with Coys. football. Semi-final B Company Competition. B Coy 1st Rounds tho. 2. A Coy 16th Batted tho. O.	
	20-12-16		Bn. carried on as per ordinary programme. Draft carried on usual instruction. Brigade Scheme without troops for officers in afternoon. CAPT. LUNN attached to 16th. Bn. Inf. Bde. for instruction.	
	21-12-16		Bn. furnished 350 men for work on ammunition dump at VALHEUREUX. Draft carried on ordinarily as per programme.	
	22-12-16		Draft handed for musketry on 30 yds range. Remainder of Bn. carried on as her programme marched to FIEFFES for baths.	
	23-12-16		2 Coys to Brigade Range, but no shooting owing to lack of targets. Remainder as per programme.	
	24-12-16		Church Parade. Cross country Road - 3 -	
	25-12-16		Attendance Drill Range.	
	26-12-16		100 men to Drill Range. 30 men musketry. Remainder as her programme. Special notice in Bn. re-organised as her new organisation. Tactical scheme without troops. Advanced guard.	
	27-12-16		Re-organisation completed. Brigade Route March and Scheme - attack in new formation.	
	28-12-16		Draft commence Part III Musketry.	
	29-12-16		Battalion carried on as her programme.	
	30-12-16		Special attention being paid to telling off large - over platoons.	
	31-12-16		Church Parade.	

CONFIDENTIAL
96/3 Vol 14

WAR DIARY.

OF

14TH BN. NORTHUMBERLAND FUSILIERS.

FROM 1ST JANUARY 1917, TO 31ST JANUARY 1917.

VOL. 14

Army Form C. 2118

WAR DIARY
or
INTELLIGENCE SUMMARY
(Erase heading not required.)

Instructions regarding War Diaries and Intelligence Summaries are contained in F.S. Regs., Part II and the Staff Manual respectively. Title Pages will be prepared in manuscript.

Place	Date	Hour	Summary of Events and Information	Remarks and references to Appendices
BONNEVILLE	1-1-17		Bn. carried on as per programme. Special Parade.	
	2-1-17		Bn. carried on as per programme. Recce Platoon in new organisation.	
	3-1-17		Draft completing musketry Part III. Remainder of Bn. carried on with programme.	
	4-1-17		Parade Special attention to new organisation.	
	5-1-17		Bn. preparing for move. Lewis Gunners, Snipers etc. picked on as rapidly as possible.	
SARTON	6-1-17		Bn. moved to SARTON.	
BUS and COUIN	7-1-17		Bn. moved. A and C Coys to BUS. B and D to COUIN. B and D Coys provided permanent working parties at COLINCAMPS and BEAUSSART and carried on with prisoners camp at BUS. A Coy carried on training on lines of new organisation.	
BUS	8-1-17		Worked tactics to show A Coy carried on as per programme. Special attention to platoon organisation. Lewis Gunnery and Bombing classes.	
	9-1-17		do	
	10-1-17		do	
	11-1-17		do	
	12-1-17		do	
	13-1-17		A Coy Coy in attack.	
			B Coy officers reconnoitred new line.	
C4	14-1-17		A Coy moving on range.	
	15-1-17		Bn. moved into trenches C4. A and C Coys in front line relieving ____ B and D Coys in support.	57d NE
COURCELLES	16-1-17		Everything extremely quiet, little or no activity. Fine. Snipers nil and Bn. mortars by gunners. Bn. relieved by 2nd R. INNIS FUS. moved to COURCELLES, in huts.	
	17-1-17		Bn. spent day cleaning up.	
	18-1-17		Bn. field use of R. Rifles.	
K 35 c 3.2 to K 36 a 45.95	19-1-17		Bn. moved into trenches occupying front from K.35.c.3.2 to K.36.a.45.95 relieving 5/6 ROYAL SCOTS and 2nd MANCHESTER REGT. B, C, D Coys in front line, A Coy in reserve. Weather extreme.	57d NE
	20-1-17		Situation quiet and normal. Patrols reported no signs of enemy on our front.	
	21-1-17		Occasional shelling of WHITE CITY by enemy. Our heavies shelled enemy near. Nothing to report. Canadian mi.	
BERTRANCOURT	22-1-17		Situation again quiet. Patrol report that enemy do not appear to be holding line in front. Bn. relieved by 15th H.L.I. moved to BERTRANCOURT into Billet. Reserve. Bn. in huts. Extreme frost.	
	23-1-17		Bn. spent day in cleaning up.	
	24-1-17		Working parties @ 1 Offr. 100th ranks BEAUSSART to R.E. @ 3 Offrs. 175th ranks to R.F.A. @ 3 Offrs. 100th ranks P.22 c central.	
	25-1-17		Working parties @ above Furnished by B, C and D Coys. A and HQ Coys carried on with	

1875 Wt. W593/827 1,000,000 4/15 J.B.C. & A. A.D.S.S./Forms/C.2118.

Army Form C. 2118

WAR DIARY
or
INTELLIGENCE SUMMARY
(Erase heading not required.)

Instructions regarding War Diaries and Intelligence Summaries are contained in F. S. Regs., Part II. and the Staff Manual respectively. Title Pages will be prepared in manuscript.

Place	Date	Hour	Summary of Events and Information	Remarks and references to Appendices
C 3	26-1-17		Bn. moved to the trenches and relieved 15th LANCS. FUS. in A,B and C3. A and B in front, C and D in support. Situation normal. Patrols sent out to get touch with enemy. Lu-Lt. Brown in charge of A Coy came under rifle and M.G. fire at K.29.d.15. No casualties.	57 d NE D2
	27-1-17		Situation normal. Patrols sent out reported no sign of enemy patrols.	
MAILLY-MAILLET	28-1-17		Situation normal. Bn. relieved by 15th LANCS. FUS. Returned to billets at MAILLY-MAILLET.	
	29-1-17		Bn. spent day in cleaning up. At night A,B and part of C Coy provided a working party to the cable trench at BEAUMONT HAMEL.	
	30-1-17		Coy training. A party of 100 other ranks reported to 32nd Div. R.A. for purpose of making a dump at P.22 central.	
	31-1-17		Company training	

Aw Littl Lieut-Col

O.C. 16th (S) Bn. North'd. Fus.

CONFIDENTIAL

Vol 15

WAR DIARY

OF

16TH (S) BN. NORTHUMBERLAND FUSILIERS

FROM 1st FEBRUARY, 1917. TO 28TH FEBRUARY, 1917.

VOL. 15.

WAR DIARY
or
INTELLIGENCE SUMMARY
(Erase heading not required.)

Army Form C. 2118

Instructions regarding War Diaries and Intelligence Summaries are contained in F.S. Regs, Part II and the Staff Manual respectively. Title Pages will be prepared in manuscript.

Place	Date	Hour	Summary of Events and Information	Remarks and references to Appendices
MAILLY MAILLET R Billeted	1-2-17		Everything forming and snowing.	57d NE
	2-2-17		The Bn was detailed to support the 9th 3rd Bde. B,C and HQ Coys moved to the line relieving the 2nd K.O.Y.L.I. in R3 subsector in front of BEAUMONT-HAMEL. HQ at WALKER QUARRY. B Coy in front holding the following posts - AXLE, HELL, HUB, WHEEL and PEACH. C Coy in support at HQ. A and D Coys remained in reserve at MAILLY MAILLET. PEACH POST was subjected to attack fire.	
	3-2-17		Returned relief took place. A and D Coys were moved to BEAUMONT-HAMEL in the morning. In the afternoon our posts and WAGON ROAD were shelled. Our own retaliated. Subsequent shelling of our posts and WAGON ROAD took place. C Coy relieved B. Patrol located enemy posts at K36 c 60.50 and K36 c 50.0.	
	4-2-17		Reported the existence of new TEN TREE ALLEY. Our front were quiet but it on being that PEACH RAID to be temporarily evacuated. When occupied it was found that the two front parts of it were unfit to be occupied. A new position was taken about distance in rear, and digging in front and rear of the garrison occupied. B Coy relieved C.	
	5-2-17		WAGON ROAD was again shelled. The position of the new post at K36 a 55.05 and D Coy were brought up from BEAUMONT HAMEL. Relief Band C. Don Jone, A in support. Bans C returning to reserve at BEAUMONT-HAMEL. Patrol again reported strong presence in TEN TREE ALLEY amongst the trees. Bn HQ having located the enemy. A Coy relieved D at night. Patrol again located enemy post near junction of TEN TREE ALLEY and WAGON ROAD and in the trees.	
	6-2-17		Enemy artillery again very active on WAGON ROAD in the morning. Increased activity in the afternoon. Our own artillery shelled the position located by the patrol. D by relieved A. The Batt. Bombers took to MAILLY-MAILLET to prepare for the attack on TEN TREE ALLEY. C Coy moved up to WALKER QUARRY.	
	7-2-17		Enemy artillery again active on WAGON ROAD. Our own shelled TEN TREE ALLEY and WHITE TRENCH. C Coy relieved D in the front line.	
	8-2-17		Enemy artillery active in the morning and evening. WAGON ROAD again subjected to heavy shelling. D Coy relieved C, the latter suffering several casualties from shell fire on returning to HQ.	
	9-2-17		In the early morning C Coy relieved D. All quiet on the morning but great activity later on in the day. A Coy under 2nd Lt TANNER, arrived at WALKER QUARRY at 4.30 p.m. At 7 p.m. the Coy moved to the tape running between AXLE and MANGO posts. At 8 p.m. the Coy was in position. Our artillery barrage opened at 8.30 p.m. when the Coy moved to the objective in TEN TREE ALLEY. It was doubted whether the operation at 9-5 p.m. Two posts were established along the front but as front could not be made with the 2nd Bn. K.O.Y.L.I. on our right and since the country had become greatly plastered, 2nd Lt BAIRD with a strong party from HUB post and reinforce the line and find front with the 13th on our right.	
	10-2-17			

WAR DIARY or INTELLIGENCE SUMMARY

Army Form C. 2118

Place	Date	Hour	Summary of Events and Information	Remarks and references to Appendices
R Beaucourt	11-2-17		At 4.40 a.m. the patrol succeeded but the R.A.F.L. were found the same distance in rear and to the right of their ground. The engineer's party, who watched from behind the line TEN TREE ALLEY, where the enemy line was found to be being wired, that it could not be penetrated. The enemy at this time also displayed great activity with rifle and M.G. fire from their strong points in the ten trees. In the afternoon about 2 o'clock an attempt was made to carry No. 5 post at K.35.C.4.2. They succeeded in dropping one or two bombs in the post, killing one man and wounding another. Eventually they were driven off with the loss of several casualties. In other quarters the enemy artillery activity prevailed throughout the day. D Coy relieved A Coy in the evening. B Coy relieved D, A relieved C at the HUB group of posts. C returned to WALKER QUARRY and D Coy went out on WAGON ROAD.	57 d NE
	12-2-17			
	13-2-17		In the morning the 17th H.L.I. attacked the strong point on TEN TREE ALLEY. The attack was preceded by a French artillery bombardment of the strong point. The attacking party were unable to make history. Our own artillery then bombarded the point during the whole of the day. Notice the enemy put up a very barrage along our front. B Coy in front suffered heavy fire from shell fire, at 10 approx our own barrage falling short. About midday Capt SMITH of our Coy. having been wounded 2nd Lt KING assumed command of the Coy. bringing with him reinforcements from A Coy. Lewis gun and rifle fire on the HUB group. Our posts kept up a heavy. The attack was however unsuccessful. In the evening the Bn. were relieved by the 2/6th W. YORKS. REGT. and returned to billets at MAILLY MAILLET and BERTRANCOURT.	
LEALVILLERS	14-2-17		Bn. moved to LEALVILLERS arriving 4.30 p.m. No men fell out on the march.	
	15-2-17		Bn. remained in billets and time spent in refitting as far as possible.	
CONTAY	16-2-17		Bn. moved to CONTAY 9 a.m. arriving about 12 noon. No men fell out on march.	
VILLERS-BOCAGE	17-2-17		Bn. moved to VILLERS-BOCAGE met 4/7 Army Corps. Gun no casualties on march.	
	18-2-17		Church parade and inspection of clothing etc. The inspector of gas helmets and the inspector of boots gave instruction throughout mornings	
	19-2-17		Bn. paraded for Physical drill, cleaning and inspection of equipment	
CAMON	20-2-17		Bn. moved to CAMON.	
BERTRANCOURT	21-2-17		B moved to BERTRANCOURT.	

WAR DIARY
or
INTELLIGENCE SUMMARY
(Erase heading not required.)

Army Form C. 2118

Instructions regarding War Diaries and Intelligence Summaries are contained in F.S. Regs., Part II. and the Staff Manual respectively. Title Pages will be prepared in manuscript.

Place	Date	Hour	Summary of Events and Information	Remarks and references to Appendices
BERTANCOURT	22-2-17		Rested at village. Time mostly devoted to anti-gas instruction and drill. Draft of 100 men to Bn.	
FRESNOY	23-2-17		Moved to FRESNOY.	
BEAUFORT	24-2-17		Bn. moved to BEAUFORT met Brigade Reserve, no K-eno notice.	
	25-2-17		Spent in reorganising Lewis Gun and Bombing teams and generally cleaning up billets & kits & arms.	
	26-2-17		Two Coys, C and D, moved into dug outs at MARVILLERS at K.12.c.0.0.	
GB.5.4.GB.1.	27-2-17		Remainder of Bn. moved into dug outs and thence to trenches at dusk to take over from 16th LANCS. FUS. in line GB5 to GB1. Disposition on line from left to right, A, B, C, D. HQ at NEY POST. Eng in wing shelled MARVILLERS – ROUVROY road and 2nd Lt ARMITAGE and C.S.M. HEBSON were wounded.	GG = NE and LL = NW
	28-2-17		Night very quiet. During day most and much work was done cleaning trenches.	

Ous Little
Lieut-Col
O.C. 16th (S) Bn Norf'k L. Inv.

WAR DIARY.

OF

16th (S) Bn. Northumberland Fusiliers.

From 1st March 1917.   To 31st March 1917.

Vol. 16.

CONFIDENTIAL.

WAR DIARY

OF

16TH (S) BN NORTHUMBERLAND FUSILIERS.

FROM 1ST MARCH 1917 TO 31ST MARCH 1917

VOL 16

Army Form C. 2118

WAR DIARY
or
INTELLIGENCE SUMMARY
(Erase heading not required.)

Instructions regarding War Diaries and Intelligence Summaries are contained in F. S. Regs., Part II and the Staff Manual respectively. Title Pages will be prepared in manuscript.

Place	Date	Hour	Summary of Events and Information	Remarks and references to Appendices
BEAUFORT	1-3-17		The day was extremely quiet. Nothing happened on front. Trenches which were bad. Bn. ordered to 10th H.L.I. and moved from Work done on Carry and to BEAUFORT.	
	2-3-17		Draft of 135 men arrived. Bn. spent time in cleaning up.	
	3-3-17		Bn. spent time in making up shortages and cleaning. Dec. ammunition inspected rifles - Favourable report.	
	4-3-17		A and B Coys proceeded for attack. C and D Coys at fighting and platoon drill. organised E 28.c. Lewis gun classes and bombing classes started.	
	5-3-17		C and D Coys carried on attack practice. A and B Coys at fighting and platoon drill. Lewis gun classes and bombing classes continued.	
	6-3-17		Bn. provided 500 men on working parties	
LE QUESNOY	7-3-17		25 men proceeded to PONT REMY on working course. Bn. again provided 200 men on working party	
	8-3-17		Bn. moved into close support to LE QUESNOY. H.Qrs. B.H.Q. LE QUESNOY, A at AUSTERLITZ, C to CASTELNAU and D to FRANCOIS WORK, relieving 15th H.L.I. Lt Col SCULLY gazetted for duty.	3 6pr + 17 LM.M. and 3 e.L.M.
	9-3-17		Bn. work on respective trenches	
	10-3-17		Bn. furnished 300 working parties on AUSTERLITZ and WAGRAM trenches. 1 Officer 1 NCO per platoon proceeded to trenches to take over.	
	11-3-17		- do -	
	12-3-17		Bn. relieved 2nd R. INNIS. FUS. in posts N of AMIENS - ROUVROY road. 3.6.p.x.17 LM.M	
	13-3-17		Extremely quiet day. on line and in support at AUSTERLITZ. Relief complete 12 midnight.	
	14-3-17		Quiet day. French raided on our right. Penetration on our 200th. Raid. - rain - trenches very bad. All went well made up of 4 officers 25 ment from 25th Infantry	
	15-3-17		5 a.m. Extremely dark and trenches bad. Bn. relieved by 2nd R. INNIS. FUS. R.Coy complete	
BOUCHOIR			Bn furnished 400 working parties. Bn. moved to BOUCHOIR	
	16-3-17		Bn. prepared to move to support attack of French S of AMIENS - ROYE road and form defensive flank. Bombs, tools etc. drawn during night.	
	17-3-17		Bn. moved from BOUCHOIR 9 a.m. to cover advance of French on right tripping by holding flank on AMIENS - ROYE road from old front line towards SE of LA CAMBUSE. French met with no Mountain and footmen encountered. Moved at 12 noon to line LA CAMBUSE - BOIS LA FUTAIE - at 9 a.m. All front line, day 5 p.m. Bn. moved into the support in old front line further. Bn. moved through PARVILLERS to line SEPT-FOURS-ETALON. Bn.Hqrs BOIS DES LATTES.	J.K.

1875 Wt. W593/826 1,000,000 4/15 J.B.C. & A. A.D.S.S./Forms/C.2118.

Army Form C. 2118

WAR DIARY
or
INTELLIGENCE SUMMARY
(Erase heading not required.)

Instructions regarding War Diaries and Intelligence Summaries are contained in F.S. Regs., Part II. and the Staff Manual respectively. Title Pages will be prepared in manuscript.

Place	Date	Hour	Summary of Events and Information	Remarks and references to Appendices
	18-3-17 contd		15th LANCS. FUS. on right. Line of old German trenches in front of wood consolidated and held during night.	
VOYENNES	19-3-17		Bn. moved at 9 a.m. through F. NESLE to position west of CANAL DU NORD with its right resting on QUIQUERY. Remained there consolidating from 12 noon until 2 p.m. when it marched to VOYENNES.	
	20-3-17		At 5.30 a.m. two companies crossed canal and Rail Line BUNY-OFFOY in conjunction with 15th LANCS. FUS. These companies were withdrawn 10 a.m. and Bn. concentrated at COURTEMANCHE	
OFFOY	21-3-17		Bn. moved to OFFOY 10 a.m. and formed defensive line N.E. of village guarding bridge head. Trenches dug on line from J.14.d.4.0. to J.14.d.4.8.	
	22-3-17		Bn. at OFFOY guarding bridge head and digging defences	
	23-3-17		— do —	
	24-3-17		— do —	
	25-3-17		— do —	
	26-3-17		— do —	
	27-3-17		— do —	
	28-3-17		— do —	
MATIGNY	29-3-17		Bn. moved at 5 a.m. to MATIGNY Billets in occu[pation]. Men employed filling in mine craters and repairing roads.	
	30-3-17		— do —	
GERMAINE	31-3-17		Bn. moved to GERMAINE. Bn. HQ at GERMAINE. 3 Coys holding outpost coast of DOUCHY-BEAUVOIS outpost line.	

Howard Cox Lt/Col
O.C.
16th Bn. Brit "L" Fus

CONFIDENTIAL.

Vol 17

WAR DIARY.

OF

16th BN. NORTHUMBERLAND FUSILIERS.

From 1st April 1917. To 30th April 1917.

Vol. 17.

CONFIDENTIAL

WAR DIARY

OF

16th Bn NORTHUMBERLAND FUSILIERS

FROM 1st APRIL 1917. TO 30th APRIL 1917.

VOL 17

WAR DIARY or INTELLIGENCE SUMMARY

Army Form C. 2118

Place	Date	Hour	Summary of Events and Information	Remarks and references to Appendices
	1-4-17		About 6 a.m. orders received to be prepared to move in view of successful attack by 97th Inf. Bde. on SAVY. At about 9 a.m. Bn. moved into forward trolley at F.13.a. reaching there 10.30 a.m. At 1.15 p.m. advance against BOIS de SAVY and wood in S.W. begun by 2nd R INNIS. FUS on right and 15th LANCS. FUS on left, Bn being in support moving in artillery formation under hostile fire. Bn reached S.W. corner of SAVY at about 2.45 p.m. and there dug in. Enemy shelled Keary and 2nd Lt DINNING wounded and 6 o.r. killed 5 o.r. wounded. Probably due to shoot observation by enemy from Cane. At 7.30 p.m. Bn moved forward into BOIS de SAVY and patrols pushed forward to HOLNON and FRANCILLY. Both found in having and forced to retire.	Ref. sheet 62 B 1 1/40000
	2-4-17		At dawn 14th Bde attacked and took point 138 and Bn moved up to take over line. The line established was point 138 to 5.21.d.2.5 and consolidation was immediately begun. 2 o.r. in front 138 to 5.21.d.4.3. (C and D) and 1 coy from 5.21.6.4.3 to 5.21.d.2.8. Casualties 8 o.r. killed 11 o.r. wounded. 1 coy in support on N.E. edge of wood. Bn. settled down to complete line of defence with strong front at point 138
	3-4-17		Day spent in consolidation. The enemy's shelling was directed on Point 138 and enemy at Staff but little damage was done. At 4.49 on the outskirts of 5.21.b between of the line. At 7 p.m. B coy relieved A coy in right sector 5.21.6.4.3. to 5.21.d.2.5. Two Lewis guns knocked out in quarry. Casualties 2 Lt WHEELDON wounded and 3 o.r. killed 4 o.r. wounded.
	4-4-17		Rainy night. At 6.30 aug. B coy being assisted by A coy. A new post was established at 5.15.d.3.7. to make better touch with 14 K.Bde.
	5-4-17 6-4-17 7-4-17		More normal days with desultory shelling mainly on point 138. Casualties were 2nd Lt WHITINGHAM slightly shell shock and 9 o.r. killed and 26 o.r. wounded. Patrols were sent out to gain enemy near ST QUENTIN and were merely fired on when about 1 mile front our line.

Army Form C. 2118

WAR DIARY
or
INTELLIGENCE SUMMARY
(Erase heading not required.)

Instructions regarding War Diaries and Intelligence Summaries are contained in F.S. Regs., Part II. and the Staff Manual respectively. Title Pages will be prepared in manuscript.

Place	Date	Hour	Summary of Events and Information	Remarks and references to Appendices
	8-4-17		Lt/Mahr (adj) Lieut Sutherin Lieut B Brown and Thomas [?] found parties the Enemy up [illegible] returned to support Coy at NE cnr of Bois de SAIX, at night on billets, more [illegible] when more brought up making 25 in all. A Coy received B Coy in front Coys right.	Re/ that 62 R
	9-4-17		Quiet. Front was now continuous threat.	40000
	10-4-17		Line established in ST QUENTIN. Remainder of day normal. Enemy returned to Bois Etang front and shelled at 5.22 & 5.25 guns and garrisoned by Hrs 1 Platoon of B Coy 10 plt's Coy. Casualties O.R. 16 killed 70 R wounded	
	11-4-17		Orders prepared to attack ST QUENTIN and if successful Bn was ordered to move with line CEPY FARM W.18 & S.16 R 2 and held it. Orders received [illegible] on 12 K S 5/6 ROYAL SCOTS (4th Bde) A and B Coys relieved at 2 a.m. C, D and HQ at 12 noon. Bn moved to GERMAINE. Throughout the period 1/4/17 - 12/4/17 the weather conditions were of the worst description and it was only by complete attention to the Person of Ely make, whole one and of hot meal every day that a great deal of sickness was prevented. Total casualties (3 Officers wounded) 23 OR killed, 6 OR missing.	40000
GERMAINE	12-4-17		Day spent in cleaning up	
	13-4-17		Orders received to move to ATKEY to support attack on FAYET.	R f.s.oo
	14-4-17		Bn moved to ATKEY and arrived there at 1 pm. Attack was postponed morning [?] 62 R Bn returned to Bivouac in GERMAINE at 4 pm as new fated.	
FAYET	15-4-17		Bn moved to HOLNON [?] relieve rmt of 14th Bde at dusk, FAYET, Bn HQ 5.5 c 9.5 with B Coy in cellars and dug outs near 67, B Coy proceeded to TWIN COPSE to support Coy of 16 R LANCS Fr's line (M.59.c)	40000
	16-4-17		Nothing to report. Bn suffered casualties HOLNON Russia.	
HOLNON	17-4-17		On night Bn must took to HOLNON in accordance with new brig of line & c one Bn in line only, Bn in support at HOLNON and two battalions in HOLNON WOOD and ATKEY. A Coy C and D at 5.3 c and 5.3 c one HQ and 1 Coy at 5.2 c. 1 Coy at TWIN COPSE remained	

WAR DIARY or INTELLIGENCE SUMMARY

Army Form C. 2118

Place	Date	Hour	Summary of Events and Information	Remarks and references to Appendices
	18/4/17 19/4/17 20/4/17		Bn. was engaged in digging and working on the BROWN LINE from Sqr. Y.9. M3d.6.9. and salvage work.	
GERMAINE ATHIES	21/4/17 21/4/17		Bn. relieved by 2/4 Oxf. Bucks. Regt. and moved to GERMAINE at 2 pm. Bn. moved to ATHIES via GUIVIERES and BUZANCOURT arriving there about 6 pm. Only two men fell out. Billets fairly good in cellars.	
	22/4/17		Cleaning up.	
	23/4/17 to 28/4/17		Training. Parties to working up, establishment of specialists. 76 Lewis Gunners, 24 Bombers, 24 Specialists in training — also 8 Lewis Gun teams, system of not less than 56 per Platoon and Section and bombers, their gunners, riflemen, rifle grenadiers.	
	29/4/17		Church Parade.	
	30/4/17		New system of organization, i.e. 25 min minimum per Platoon and maximum 50 men and 2 or 4 Platoons per Coy. Section organization the same, i.e. 1 Platoon must have not less than 25 men, not more than 50. 1 Coy with 100 men = 4 Platoons = 2 Platoons with 50, 1 Coy.	

J. Knocke Capt.
O. Commanding 16th Bn. Royal d. Fus.

CONFIDENTIAL

Vol 18

WAR DIARY.

of

16TH (S) Bn. NORTHUMBERLAND FUSILIERS

FROM 1ST MAY 1917 To 31ST MAY 1917.

VOL. XVIII.

WAR DIARY
or
INTELLIGENCE SUMMARY

(Erase heading not required.)

Army Form C. 2118

Instructions regarding War Diaries and Intelligence Summaries are contained in F. S. Regs., Part II. and the Staff Manual respectively. Title Pages will be prepared in manuscript.

Place	Date	Hour	Summary of Events and Information	Remarks and references to Appendices
ATHIES	1-5-17 to 15		Bn. remained at ATHIES training. Particular attention was paid to form of attack over open and front to place to front. Specialists i.e. Rifle grenadiers, Bombers, Lewis Gunners and signallers were trained up to establishment and 100% over.	
	16-5-17		During the period Bn. was made up to strength of 700 at all ranks with 8th Bn. Transport exceptionally fit and well.	
OMIECOURT	16-5-17		Bn. moved from ATHIES to OMIECOURT en route to join 14th CORPS	
ROSIERES	17-5-17		Bn. moved to ROSIERES and CHAULNES	
	18-5-17		Orders to remain at ROSIERES and carry out training. There were received. Message received from G.O.C. 4th ARMY thanking Division for work done and wishing Bn. luck in new corps.	
	19-5-17 to 28-5-17		Bn. carried on training in same lines as before. Lord Nelson's was done on the ranges. Much shooting being encouraged.	
	29-5-17		Bde. Sports were held. Bn. doing well and carrying off 8 firsts in 23 events	
GUILLAUCOURT	30-5-17		Bn. moved to GUILLAUCOURT in order to concentrate for Bde. entrainment to CAESTRE.	
	31-5-17		Training and preparing for entrainment on 1st June.	

Thanks Cope but
F. G. Commanding
16th (S)Bn. North'd Fus

CONFIDENTIAL.

Vol 19

WAR DIARY

OF

16TH (S) Bn. NORTHUMBERLAND FUSILIERS

FROM 1ST JUNE 1917.   TO 30TH JUNE 1917.

VOL XIX.

Army Form C. 2118

WAR DIARY
or
INTELLIGENCE SUMMARY
(Erase heading not required.)

Instructions regarding War Diaries and Intelligence Summaries are contained in F. S. Regs., Part II. and the Staff Manual respectively. Title Pages will be prepared in manuscript.

Place	Date	Hour	Summary of Events and Information	Remarks and references to Appendices
BLEU	1-6-17		Strength 34 Officers 737 other ranks.	
	2-6-17	7 a.m.	Bn. entrained for CAESTRE arriving at 6.30 p.m. Marched to billets in BLEU.	
	5-6-17		Bn. trained by Coys. Ground attention to musketry and Gas respirator drill.	
	6-6-17			
	7-6-17		2nd Army attack on MESSINES ridge. 32nd Division in support to 2nd ANZAC CORPS. The attack was everywhere successful and the Division was not called on.	
	8-6-17		Bn. remained prepared for movement. Called on R.Q.M.S. Armstrong was decorated with D.C.M. for work at BEAUMONT HAMEL on 13/11. G.O.C. 2nd Lt Tarmachill joined for duty.	
	9-6-17		Routine work and ordinary training was carried on.	
	10-6-17		Church Parades.	
	11-6-17			
STEENVORDE	12-6-17		Training. The following Officers reported for duty. 2nd Lt. T.V. WHEGELDON, 2nd Lt. J.H. FAULDER, 2nd Lt. KANISTER, 2nd Lt. W.S. WAGER, and a draft of 107 other ranks arrived.	
	13-6-17		Bn. left BLEU at 6 a.m. and marched to camp near STEENVORDE arriving 10.15 a.m. Very hot and dusty. 2nd Lt. R.A. LAMARQUE reported for duty.	
WORMHOUDT	13-6-17		Bn. marched from camp near STEENVORDE at 7 a.m. and reached WORMHOUDT at 10 a.m. Men billeted in farms.	
	14-6-17		Bn. remained in Billets at WORMHOUDT.	
MALO-BAINS	15-6-17		An advance party of Officers and N.C.O.s left by bus at 7 a.m. to reconnoitre approach and front line.	
	16-6-17		The Bn. entrained at 7.30 a.m. at LEFFERINGCOUCHE and detrained at OOST- DUNKERQUE STN. BELGIUM. Confusion first as to ambulance. At 10 p.m. the Bn. moved off to the support line W of Coxyde and S.E. of NIEUPORT- BAINS, and took over from the 2nd ROYAL Infantry Regiment (41). A, B and D Coys in support line. C Coy billeted in JEANNIOT CAMP, COXYDE.	Pte 19 1/40.0.E
	17-6-17		Bn. in support line. Draft of 13 other ranks arrived.	
	18-6-17	10.30 pm	A, B and D Coys moved across canal and took over front line from French. A Coy on right, B Coy on left and D Coy in support. No casualties during relief. C Coy in camp at COXYDE. Front of 800 yards. 15th LANCS. FUS. on left, 14 Bt. BRIGADE on right.	
	19-6-17		In front line. Shelled at intervals during day. Some M.G. fire during night. No casualties. 2nd Lt. F.T. ROBINSON reported for duty.	
	20-6-17		Holding front line. Fairly heavy shelling of intervals at Wiltorman during the day	

WAR DIARY or INTELLIGENCE SUMMARY

(Erase heading not required.)

Army Form C. 2118

Place	Date	Hour	Summary of Events and Information	Remarks and references to Appendices
	21-6-17		At 1 a.m. the enemy placed a barrage of 77 m.m and 105 m.m. trench mortars and rifle grenades on our 1st and 2nd lines and C.T's. after a few minutes of which from our front line trench and was answered on the 2nd line and C.T.'s. Simultaneously afterwards an enemy raiding party entered our front trench in a 67 packet and was successful in gaining an entrance. The enemy men were many. The enemy remained only a few minutes in our trench. The barrage continued until 1.30 a.m when it slackened and at 1.55 a.m it had ceased. During the day the enemy was observed somewhat heavy at intervals. In the afternoon a rifle bullet close to the entrance of Bn H.Q. and wounded 2nd Lt. R.C.MILES and 3 Otherranks. Cpl. T.M.HAKE was also hit dy y(?) Some M.G. fire but machine dropping during the night. Days of 4 otherranks since Bn.	BELGIUM No. 19. 1/40,000
COXYDE	22-6-17		Sleeping front line. Manual shelling during the day and some M.G. fire at night. Between 10-5 p.m and 10.35 p.m the enemy placed on line heavy. Phosporous in retaliation for the activity of our guns earlier in the evening	
	23-6-17		On front line. Manual shelling during the day. During the night of the 23/24 it was received by the 1st R. BERKS. REGT. Relief effected about 9 A.B and D Coys marched to camp at COXYDE. C & m Coys by 8 a.m. 24/6/17	
	24-6-17		Generally whilst in the trenches: 2nd Lt R.C.MILES and 2nd Lt W.HAMILTON Flear otherranks (the later officer during the raid on the morning of the 21st) otherranks wounded. Three O.R killed. nineteen O.R wounded.	
CHYVELDE	25-6-17		During the 24th the Bn rested in camp. The Bn. left JEANNIOT CAMP. COXYDE at 5 a.m and marched to CHYVELDE.	
	26-6-17		Men in huts. Officers billeted in village. Training	

Army Form C. 2118

WAR DIARY
or
INTELLIGENCE SUMMARY
(Erase heading not required.)

Instructions regarding War Diaries and Intelligence Summaries are contained in F. S. Regs., Part II. and the Staff Manual respectively. Title Pages will be prepared in manuscript.

Place	Date	Hour	Summary of Events and Information	Remarks and references to Appendices
GHYVELDE	27-6-17		Training. CAPT. T.H. WAKE went on leave 2nd Lt F.H. WORTHINGTON acting as adjutant during his absence.	
	28-6-17		Training	
	29-6-17		Training	
	30-6-17		Training. Bn carried out attack practice.	

F H Worthy W J Lt o/a/ady for Lt-Col.
Commanding 16th (S) Bn. Norfolk Regt.

1875 Wt. W593/826 1,000,000 4/15 J.B.C. & A. A.D.S.S./Forms/C. 2118.

Confidential

Vol 20

War Diary of 16th (S) Bn.
Northumberland Fusiliers,
from 1st July 1917 to 31st July 1917.

Vol. XX.

WAR DIARY or INTELLIGENCE SUMMARY

Army Form C. 2118

Place	Date	Hour	Summary of Events and Information	Remarks and references to Appendices
GHYVELDE.	1/7/17		Sunday. Brigade Church Parade.	
	2/7/17		Brigade carried out a practice attack on a system of trenches representing a section of the enemy line at LOMBARTZYDE.	
	3/7/17		Brigade practice attack repeated.	
	4/7/17		The Battalion left GHYVELDE at 6-30 a.m. and marched to TEARNIYOT CAMP near COXYDE 2 arriving 10 a.m. The Battalion remained in Camp for the rest of the day.	
NIEUPORT.	5/7/17		Advance parties of Officers and N.C.Os. went to NIEUPORT during the day. H.M. the KING passed the Camp at 2 p.m. At 8.30 p.m. "A" "B" and "D" Companies marched to NIEUPORT and relieved the 15th HIGH. L.I. Relief complete by 12.30 a.m. 6.7.17. No casualties. "C" Company behind at GROOT LABEUR FARM. Battalion in Divisional reserve. "A" "B" and "D" Companies in cellars in NIEUPORT.	
	6/7/17		NIEUPORT shelled at intervals during the hours of daylight. Very little shelling at night. Patrols out after dark reconnoitring "no mans land", in front of the enemy 2 trenches selected for the raid. "C" Company behind in training for the raid.	
	7/7/17		More Patrols out at night. The point selected for the raid was the enemy block-house and trenches between the canal and creek in M.24.d.	
	8/7/17		Rain most of the day. Patrols out again at night.	
	9/7/17		Usual night Patrols. No hill the morning of the 10th there was only moderate shelling of NIEUPORT during daylight and as a rule the nights were quiet. "A" Company commanded by Capt. E.H. LUCETTE, "B" Company by Capt L.B. PROCTOR and "D" Company by 2/Lieut. R. McLEAN (in the absence of Capt. C.F. MAYOS, on leave) "C" Company commanded by Lieut. J. WATSON. 2/Lieut. F.H. WORTHINGTON acting Adjutant.	

WAR DIARY
or
INTELLIGENCE SUMMARY

Army Form C. 2118

Place	Date	Hour	Summary of Events and Information	Remarks and references to Appendices
NIEUPORT.	10/7/17		Enemy bombardment started at 6 a.m. and increased gradually in intensity until 9 a.m. Early in the forenoon all wires were cut and no information came through, but from observation it was seen that the area bombarded extended from the Coast of NIEUPORT. To the night of NIEUPORT the shelling was normal. In the afternoon the Battalion came under the orders of the 97th Brigade. Men standing-to in cellars. In the evening "C" Company was brought up to the road junction 300× West of NIEUPORT to await orders. While moving up they came under heavy shell fire and had about 30 casualties. About 10 p.m. orders were received to man the NIEUPORT defences. "A", "B" and "D" Companies moved into position in the trenches lining the West bank of the canal. "C" Company came up and occupied the billets vacated by "B" Company. At this time the enemy were sending over gas shells. 2/Lieut. F.W. STONE and 2/Lieut. F. AMSTEY and a number of men were gassed. 2/Lieut. L.T. MANN was killed by shell fire. About 2 a.m. in accordance with further orders received the Companies closed and crossed the canal to relieve the 11/2 Border Regt holding the front line. The relief was complete by 6 a.m. and patrols were pushed out to ascertain the exact position of the enemy who had captured the front and second lines of the Borden's Point. 2/Lieut. M.F. PEYTON killed, 2/Lieut. W.S. WAGER wounded and missing. "A" Company on left, "D" Company on right. "C" Company in Reserve in	
	11/7/17		NIEUPORT. The very heavy shelling of the previous day had slackened off at dusk, but NIEUPORT and the trenches East of it were subjected to fairly heavy bombardments at intervals during the 11/2. In the afternoon, orders having been received to recapture the lost trenches, "A" Company formed up to attack but came under heavy and accurate fire and suffered severe casualties. The attack was postponed until dark when "C" Company was brought up and relieved "A" Company. At 10.30 p.m. the enemy attacked on "D" Company's	
	12/7/17		front and were repulsed. At 1.45 a.m. "D" Company on the right and "C" Company on	

WAR DIARY
or
INTELLIGENCE SUMMARY

(Erase heading not required.)

Army Form C. 2118

Place	Date	Hour	Summary of Events and Information	Remarks and references to Appendices
NIEUPORT	12/7/17		and in rear of 'D' Company were formed up ready to attack. 'C' Company moved forward, but came under heavy Machine gun and Rifle fire from the left which inflicted severe losses and prevented further advance. As they did not reach the line held by 'D' Company the attack by the latter Company could not be carried out. Both 'B' Company Officers advancing with the attack – 2/Lieut. N.T. FUTERS and 2/Lieut. T.V. WHEELDON – were wounded. In the early hours of the morning the Battalion was relieved by the 5/6th ROYAL SCOTS Regt and moved back into cellars in NIEUPORT standing to prepared to man the NIEUPORT defences. During the night of the 11th/12th NIEUPORT and the canal were heavily bombarded with Lachrymatory and gas shells. In the early morning of the 12th the 97th Brigade was relieved by the 14th Brigade and the Battalion came under the orders of the latter. From the morning of the 11th until the morning of the 12th Col. A.J. SCULLY, M.C. had under his command three Companies of the 11th HIGH. L.I. and one Company of the 2nd K.O.Y.L.I. During the 12th the Battalion remained in Billets in NIEUPORT. At night it was relieved by the 1st DORSET Regt and moved back to "A" BAILLET CAMP East of OOST-DUNKERQUE.	
	13/7/17		The Battalion rested in camp. Casualties 11 Officers 240 other ranks during operations. On "A" BAILLET CAMP.	
	14/7/17		In camp until 9-15 p.m. when the Battalion marched back to NIEUPORT and relieved the 13th Lanc. Fus. In billets by 1 a.m. On the night of the 16th 'B' Company crossed the canal and were in support to the 1st DORSET Regt for some hours, then returned to Billets.	
	15/7/17			
	16/7/17			
	17/7/17		NIEUPORT shelled lightly at intervals.	
	18/7/17		At night the Battalion was relieved by the 1/8 W. YORK. R. and marched to JEANNIOT CAMP, COXYDE. All in camp by 3 a.m.	
	19/7/17		Capt. W. A. GOSS joined for duty. In camp.	

Army Form C. 2118

WAR DIARY
or
INTELLIGENCE SUMMARY
(Erase heading not required.)

Instructions regarding War Diaries and Intelligence Summaries are contained in F. S. Regs., Part II. and the Staff Manual respectively. Title Pages will be prepared in manuscript.

Place	Date	Hour	Summary of Events and Information	Remarks and references to Appendices
	20/7/17		Draft of 52 men arrived.	
	21/7/17		Draft of 186 men arrived.	
	22/7/17		Sunday. Church Parades.	
In JERNIOT CAMP.	23/7/17		do	
	24/7/17		do	
	25/7/17		While in JERNIOT CAMP the Battalion furnished large working and carrying parties by day and night and there was very little time for training. In the afternoon of the 26th the Battalion marched by Companies to BRAY DUNES. Officers in billets in the village, three Companies in tents and one Company in billets. The Battalion took over the Coast Defences of the BRAY DUNES Sector.	
	26/7/17			
	27/7/17		The day was spent in cleaning up. The C.O. and Company Commanders reconnoitred the Coast Defences.	
	28/7/17		Training started.	
	29/7/17		Sunday. Church Parades.	
	30/7/17		Training and Working Parties.	
	31/7/17		The Battalion marched from BRAY DUNES at 6.20 a.m. and reached COXYDE at 9.20 a.m. Officers billeted in village - men bivouaced in field.	

CONFIDENTIAL

Vol 21

WAR DIARY

of

16th Bn Northumberland Fusiliers

from 1st August, 1917   to   31st August 1917

Vol. XXI.

WAR DIARY or INTELLIGENCE SUMMARY

Army Form C. 2118.

(Erase heading not required.)

Instructions regarding War Diaries and Intelligence Summaries are contained in F. S. Regs., Part II. and the Staff Manual respectively. Title pages will be prepared in manuscript.

Place	Date	Hour	Summary of Events and Information	Remarks and references to Appendices
COXYDE	1/8/17		Heavy rain during night and all day. Bn marched to RIBAILLET CAMP near OOST DUNKERKE. In the evening the Bn marched to RIBAILLET CAMP.	BELGIUM. Sheet 11. 1/40,000 X 13 a.
OOST DUNKERKE	2·8·17		Bn in RIBAILLET CAMP. Rain during day. Parties of officers & N.C.O's reconnoitred right sub-sector. ST. GEORGES.	R. 36. C
	3·8·17		Rain. In the evening "B", "C" & "D" coys relieved the 16th Lancs Fus. in left subsector, ST. GEORGES. B"&"C"Coys in the front line, "D" coy in support. Bn. H.Q. at BRIQUETERIE. "A" coy remained at RIBAILLIET CAMP.	
Trenches ST GEORGES Left Subsector	4·8·17		Rain. Intervals of heavy shelling during the day. Short intervals of heavy shelling during the night. Patrols out at night in front of RAT POST. The following officers joined for duty. 2nd Lt C. BUGLASS. 2nd Lt H. ALLINSON. 2nd Lt R. WATGOTT. 2nd Lt R. TAYLOR. G. C. W. PRINGLE. J. T. SMALLWOOD. J. R. STEVENSON.	BELGIUM. Sheet 12. 1/20,000 S.W. - 1/20,000
"	5·8·17		Fairly heavy shelling at intervals. During the night the enemy continued the 10 to 15 minute bombardments at Nieuport Ammo-Polard out in front of RAT POST.	M 24 d 4.4
"	6·8·17		At 1·45 am a raiding party of 15 men and 1 M.G.O. under 2nd Lt TOWNSEND, from "C" Coy advanced under a barrage and entered RAT TRENCH. Several enemies found in the trench were killed, but no prisoners were secured. The party remained in the enemy trench for 20 mins. Our casualties were 2nd Lt TOWNSEND and 14 O.R. wounded. In the evening "C" coy was relieved by "D" coy and "B" Coy by "A". Naval patrols out at night.	
"	7·8·17		The front and support trenches were heavily shelled. "A" coy having about 40 casualties in the two platoons holding the front line. Operation Orders for a raid by "D" coy and one platoon of "A" coy had been issued and the scheme explained verbally by the C.O. to the officers and N.C.O's concerned. In view of "A" coy casualties most of which had occurred in the platoon selected for the raid and the difficulties of reorganising in the short time available it was proposed by the B.O. and approved by Brigade that the raid should be carried out by "D" coy only. At night the forming up line in NO MAN'S LAND was taped out.	
"	8·8·17		At 12·45 am "D" Coy was formed up ready to advance. The barrage which was very good started at 1·00am. The coy immediately advanced and succeeded in entering RAT POST and RAT TRENCH. the bombing squads pushing forward some 60 yds down the C.T.'s towards RAVEN TRENCH. Only three enemies were found, who, because they resisted, were killed, but before and letters taken from them furnished the identification required. The raiding company remained in the enemy lines until 1·40am. The attack and return was carried out in exceptionally good order. Our casualties	

A 5834 Wt. W4973/M687 750,000 8/16 D. D. & L. Ltd. Forms/C.2118/13

WAR DIARY
or
INTELLIGENCE SUMMARY.
(Erase heading not required.)

Army Form C. 2118.

Instructions regarding War Diaries and Intelligence Summaries are contained in F. S. Regs., Part II. and the Staff Manual respectively. Title pages will be prepared in manuscript.

Place	Date	Hour	Summary of Events and Information	Remarks and references to Appendices
Thumbut ST GEORGES Sector (left)	8-8-17		2nd Lt. STEVENSON killed and 29 O.R. killed, wounded and missing. Capt. Mayes commanded the Bompany. In the afternoon and evening Bn. Hd. Qrs at the BRIQUETERIE were heavily shelled by 7.5" hour. causing casualties. During the night the enemy continued to bombard the lines & shut intervals at irregular times. Naval shelling during the day. At night the Bn. was relieved by the 16th Lanc. Fus., and marched back to RIBAILLET CAMP. Total Casualties between 3rd and 9th August:— 2nd Lt STEVENSON killed 8-8-17, and Lt. ROBINSON, wounded. 2nd Lt F.R. COLLINS wounded (at duty) 15 O.R. killed, 86 O.R. wounded, 3 O.R. wounded & missing, 5 O.R. missing.	BELGIUM Sheet 12 S.W./NIEUPORT M 29 C 4 5.
	9-8-17		Am in RIBAILLET CAMP. Working parties in the line by night.	
RIBAILLET CAMP	10-8-17		do	
"	11-8-17		do	
"	12-8-17		do	
"	13-8-17		2nd Lt F.W. RIDLEY joined for duty. Draft of 23 O.R. arrived	
"	14-8-17		2nd Lt. A.G. KING joined Bn.	
"	15-8-17		In RIBAILLET CAMP. Working parties furnished at night. Lieuts W.R. SLACK, T.W. THOMPSON and A. WATTS joined for duty.	
"	16-8-17		Enemy bombarded Camp with 400 shells 2nd Day until 2:30 am when Bn. marched to COYDE. 33rd Div. relieved by 32nd Div. Draft of 35 O.R. joined	BELGIUM Sheet 11 1/40,000 X.13.C.
"	17-8-17		In RIBAILLET CAMP. 2nd Lts. E.H. GOWDY, W. BOLAM, W.D. SMART, joined for duty.	
"	18-8-17		In camp until 2.30 pm when the Bn. marched to COXYDE. 3rd Bn. relieved by 3 Bn.-	FRANCE Sheet 19 1/40000 D.9.C.
COXYDE	19-8-17		Draft of 35 O.R. joined	
BRAY DUNES	19-8-17		Bn. left COXYDE and marched to BRAY DUNES. Draft of 18 O.R. joined	
"	20-8-17		Sunday. Church Parades. Draft of 38 O.R. joined	
"	21-8-17		Training commenced	
"	22-8-17		Training	
"	23-8-17		Training	
"	24-8-17		Training. Draft of 9 O.R. joined	
"	25-8-17		Training	
"	26-8-17		Sunday. Church Parades.	
"	27-8-17		Training	
"	28-8-17		Training	
COYDE	29-8-17	9.30 am	Bn. marched to CANADA CAMP (Colt. JEANNIOT CAMP) COXYDE on CANADA CAMP. Training. "A" Coy attached 259 Tunnelling Coy. R.E. COXYDE BAINS	BELGIUM Sheet 11 1/40,000 W.18.6.
"	30-8-17		do	
"	31-8-17		do	

A 5834 Wt W4973/M687 750,000 8/16 D. D. & L. Ltd. Forms/C. 2118/13.

CONFIDENTIAL

WA 23.
22

War Diary
of
16th (S) Bn. Northumberland Fusiliers

Vol XXII.

16 North F-Us — 1st to 30th Sep 17. SHEET 1.

Army Form C. 2118

WAR DIARY or **INTELLIGENCE SUMMARY**

(Erase heading not required.)

Instructions regarding War Diaries and Intelligence Summaries are contained in F. S. Regs., Part II. and the Staff Manual respectively. Title Pages will be prepared in manuscript.

Place	Date 1917	Hour	Summary of Events and Information	Remarks and references to Appendices
COXYDE.	1. Sept.		Bn. in CANADA CAMP, COXYDE. Large working and carrying parties were furnished, chiefly by night. During our in trenches trouble.	
	2.		Do.	BELGIUM
	3.		Do.	
	4.		Do. — At night a party of officers went up to the line to reconnoitre the LOMBARTZYDE SECTOR.	SHEET II.
	5.		Do. — and lines were further reconnoitred.	
	6.		Do.	
	7.		Do. — Draft of 6 O.R. arrived.	1/40.000
	8.		In CANADA CAMP. At 4.50 am. a shell from a H.V. gun struck the hut occupied as Bn HQ. and wounded Capt. T. KILLATT (RAMC attached) seriously, and Major A. ARCHER slightly. 2/Lieut C. S. SUTHERLAND found fit for duty. Capt. D. LINDSAY took over command of 4 Bn. from Major A. ARCHER.	K.I.18.B
	9.		Do. { 2/Lt A. WILLIAMSON } found fit for duty. { S. J. HENDERSON }	
	10.		Do. J. H. GREEN Rejoined — Grenade struck 32 Dn. T.M.B	
	11.		Do. During the time the Bn. was in the trenches an enemy H.V. gun shelled COXYDE and AUSTRALIA and CANADA Camps occasionally for short periods chiefly at night. a few shells fell in the camps but the only casualties caused were three (Nature returned) on morning of 8 Sept.	

{ 2nd Lieut. D. DAVIDSON, H. A. DODDS, L. R. CHEVREAU and draft of 8 O.R. joined for duty. }

16 NORTH'D FUS.   1 - 30 SEP.T 17   Army Form C. 2118

WAR DIARY
or
INTELLIGENCE SUMMARY
(Erase heading not required.)

SHEET 2.

Place	Date 1917	Hour	Summary of Events and Information	Remarks and references to Appendices
LOMBARTZYDE Right sub sector E. of CANAL	12-Sep.		At 11pm, the Bn. marched from CANADA CAMP and took over the line in the LOMBARTZYDE Right sub. sector from 5/6th ROYAL SCOTS. Disposition on completion of relief :— B.C. on right, E.C. on left, A.C. in support, and D.C. in reserve. Ill East of Canal.	BELGIUM SHEET. 12.S.W. 1/20,000
	13		On the line. Fairly heavy shelling at intervals. Principally with T.M.'s. At night the lines and C.T.s have caught with bursts of M.G. fire.	
	14		— Do — — do —	
	15		— Do — — do —	
	16		At dawn on the morning of the 16th the enemy turned an Artillery and T.M. barrage on the R2 and 3 F lines under cover of which a small raiding party entered the just line trench at the junction of "B" and "C" Co. frontage. She left post of "B" Co. and all became casualties from T.M.'s. She raiding party was driven to the middle with rifle and and thus grenade out of the enemy party led his rig and was to the middle until fired on by the canyons of the trench and thrust post. Some their own lines. One man of the enemy party left his rig and was shot in our second line. On returning, the raiders stood to fire I. OR are Artillery barrage. Our casualties from the raid were :— I. OR missing (believed P.W. A), 5. OR. OR. in A. and 11. OR. wounded.	M.23.D.
NEWPORT.	17."		On the night of the 17/18 the Bn. was relieved by the 2nd R. INNIS. FUS. and went into reserve at NEWPORT. Bn. H.Q and D.C. in NEW PARADE, D.C finding the garrison for PRESQUILLE. A.B. and C Co. in NEWPORT.	M.27.B
	18.		On its arrival, Entering and Northn. Patrol in the line at night. Draft of 16 OR. came up to Batn.	

16 NORTH'D FUS.

WAR DIARY — 1-30 SEPT 17.
INTELLIGENCE SUMMARY   SHEET. 3.

Army Form C. 2118

Place	Date 1917	Hour	Summary of Events and Information	Remarks and references to Appendices
NIEUPORT.	19 Sept		On Reserve. Carrying parties and working parties in the line at night.	BELGIUM, SHEET 12 SW 40,000
	20		— Do — do —	M. 27. B.
LOMBARTZYDE Right Sub Sect E. of CANAL.	21		At night the Bn. crossed the Canal and relieved the 2nd R. INNIS. FUS in the LOMBARTZYDE Right Sub. sector. 'A' Coy on right, 'D' Coy on left, 'C' Coy in support and 'B' in reserve.	M. 23. D.
	22		Bn. in the line. Shelling and random gun fire active. Cmdt. Lucas wounded. 2 kindly shelled by T.M.s.	
	23		— Do —	
	24		— do —	Capt. E. HESTERLOW R.A.M.C. attached for duty.
NIEUPORT.	24		On the night of the 24th the Bn. was relieved by the 2nd R. INNIS. FUS. and went back into reserve in NEW PARADE at NIEUPORT.	2 Lieut. G. HARMAN J. WALLER joined for duty from 49. OTB.
	25		— Do —	Lieut. Col. A.J. SCULLY returned from leave and took over
	26			Bn. from Capt. LINDSAY
	27		On Reserve. Working and carrying parties at night.	
COXYDE.	28		On the night of the 28th the Bn was relieved by the 1st/6th HIGH. L.I. and marched back to CANADA CAMP, COXYDE.	BELGIUM SHEET 12 40,000 W. 18. B.
	29		In Camp. Men cleaning up. Large working parties at night.	

16 North'd Fus.

WAR DIARY
or
INTELLIGENCE SUMMARY
(Erase heading not required.)

Army Form C. 2118

1 to 30 Sept. 17. SHEET. 4.

Place	Date 1917	Hour	Summary of Events and Information	Remarks and references to Appendices
Coxyde.	30 Sep		On Canada Camp. The Battalion casualties during the last tour in the trenches, were:— 2nd Lieut. H. Allinson Wounded. 19.9.17. " W. Bolay " " " F.R. Cowings do 21.9.17. 10 O.R. O.R. w.i.a. 57 " " Wounded 1 " " Missing.	BELGIUM SHEET 11 40,000. W 18.9.

On the Field.
1st Oct 1/

O. Dudley Quick Lieut.
Comm: 16(S) Bn. North'd Fus.

16 North Fus.

War Diary

1st to 30th Sept '17.

Vol XXII

Confidential

Confidential

Vol #23

War Diary
of
16th Bn: Northumberland Fusiliers

1st to 31st October 1917.

Vol XXIII.

16th Bn: NORTHUMBERLAND FUSILIERS. WAR DIARY 1st to 31st OCTOBER 1917. Army Form C. 2118.

INTELLIGENCE SUMMARY.

SHEET 1.

Place	Date 1917.	Hour	Summary of Events and Information	Remarks and references to Appendices
COXYDE.	1 Oct.		Camp. Camp warfare tactics by day and night. Capt T.H.WHITE took over duties on 96th Infantry Brigade Staff., and Capt. E.H. LUCETTE became Acting Adjutant.	BELGIUM SHEET 11. 1/40,000
	2		At 6.30 P.M. the Bn. left CANADA CAMP, COXYDE, and marched to LA PANNE, taking over billets from the 2nd Bn. R. INNIS. FUS.	W.18.B.
LA PANNE.	3		In LA PANNE. Men in rests. Officers in houses in the town.	
	4		Do. Do.	
	5		The Bn. left LA PANNE at 9 A.M. 2nd Lieut F. DAWSON joined for duty (from 17 Bn NORTH.FUS). and marched along the sands to FORT DE DUNES, taking over the Coast Defence and billets from the 11th Bn THE QUEEN'S. The Company Officers and men in low huts, H.Q. Officers in billets.	Do. Do. W.14.15.
FORT DES DUNES.	6		At FORT DE DUNES. Coll. and out.	Do SHEET 19 C. central.
	7	SUNDAY	Do. Church Parade.	
	8		Do. Practice manning of the Coast Defences. Training.	
	9		Do.	
	10		Do.	
	11		Do. Capt. E.H. LUCETTE left for ENGLAND on one months leave. 2nd Lieut F.H. WORTHINGTON acting Adjutant.	
	12		Do.	
	13		Do.	
	14		Do.	
	15		Do.	
	16		Do. 2nd Lieut F. DAWSON proceeded to join 1/6 Bn NORTH. FUS.	

16 Bn. North'd Fus. 1-31st Oct 17.   SHEET 2.

Army Form C. 2118.

WAR DIARY
or
INTELLIGENCE SUMMARY.
(Erase heading not required.)

Instructions regarding War Diaries and Intelligence Summaries are contained in F. S. Regs., Part II. and the Staff Manual respectively. Title pages will be prepared in manuscript.

Place	Date 1917	Hour	Summary of Events and Information	Remarks and references to Appendices
FORT DE DUNES	17 Oct.		At FORT DE DUNES	BELGIUM AND FRANCE SHEET 19. C central.
	18		Do.	
	19		Do.	
	20		Do. The Brigade carried out a practice attack. 2nd Lieut. W.L.C. HUTTON reported for duty.	
	21		Do.	
	22		Do.	
	23		Do.	
	24		Do.	
TETEGHEM.	25		The Bn. marched to TETEGHEM.	Do. 1. 15 central.
ZEGGERS CAPPEL	26		The Bn. marched to ZEGGERS CAPPEL.	
	27		ZEGGERS CAPPEL. Sunday. Officers and men billeted in farms outside village. Church Parades.	
	28		Do. Training.	
	29		Parties of Officers reconnoitred approaches to front line WEST of POELCAPPELLE.	
	30		Do. do.	
	31		Do. do. 9th Inf. Bde. inspected by Divisional General.	

In the field.
1st November 1917.

[signature]
C.O. 16 (S) Bn Northumberland Fusiliers.

Confidential

WAR DIARY.

of

16th Bn. Northumberland Fusiliers

1st to 30th November, 1917

Vol. XXIV

"A" Form.
MESSAGES AND SIGNALS.

Army Form C. 2121.
(In pads of 100.)

TO: 32nd Division.

Sender's Number.	Day of Month.	In reply to Number.	AAA
BM 152	13	A 225	

Herewith War Diary of 16th Bn Northumberland Fusiliers for month of November.

W. Girdwood
Brig Gen
Commanding
96th Inf Bde

WAR DIARY
or
INTELLIGENCE SUMMARY.

(Erase heading not required.)

Army Form C. 2118.

Vol 24

Place	Date 1917	Hour	Summary of Events and Information	Remarks and references to Appendices
ZEGGERS CAPPEL	10/11		Battalion in billets at ZEGGERS CAPPEL. Training etc	FRANCE & BELGIUM Sheet 27.
	11th		Bn. marched to billets at LEDRINGHAM	
LEDRINGHAM	12th		Bn. marched to camp in WINNIZEELE area.	1 in J.M. and C. Sheet 28.C.15.c
Sheet 27. J.12.c	13th		Bn. entrained at WINNIZEELE to ESSEX FARM. and marched to camp near TURCO FARM	" " "
TURCO FARM	14/22nd		A, B, & C Coys. provided working parties for C.R.A. 'D' Coy provided working parties for C.R.E. H.Q. Details erected NISSEN Huts in camp.	
	23rd		Bn. marched to DRAKE CAMP (huts)	Sheet 28. A 30.c
DRAKE CAMP	24/27		Bn in huts. Reconnoitring parties sent to line.	
	28th		Bn entrained at DIRTY BUCKET to MERRYTHOUGHT (WIELTJE) and marched from there to bivouacs at WURST FARM.	" " 3rd
WURST FARM	29th		Advance parties proceeded to line.	
	30th		Bn. took over line from 2nd R. Irwin two Bn H.Q. at MEETCHEELE Bn. of 8th Sinclair on right. 15th Hants two on left.	" 0 Sept

Mmath Capt.
15 Nov 17.

CONFIDENTIAL

WA 25

War Diary
of
Lt. Gen. Northumberland Division
1st to 31st December 97.

Volume XXV

CONFIDENTIAL

War Diary
of
1st Bn Northumberland
Fusiliers
1st to 31st December 1914

France.

XXV

WAR DIARY or INTELLIGENCE SUMMARY

Army Form C. 2118

1/F. Bn. Northumberland Fusiliers

1st to 31st December 1917

Place	Date	Hour	Summary of Events and Information	Remarks and references to Appendices
	1st Dec 1917		Bn on right of Divisional Sector holding line from South of TEALL COT through VOCATION and VIRILE FARMS. During the early morning of the 1st Dec., Lieut. C.S. SUTHERLAND and one platoon of 'A' Coy. attempted to capture TEALL COT but were met by heavy M.G. fire and could not advance — Casualties 2/Lieut SUTHERLAND and 8 O.R. At 5.15 A.M. C Lieut. I to T the enemy attacked on the left but were easily repulsed. Civis Gunn and rifle fire. C and D Coys later in the day one unsuccessful prisoner was brought in at Coy Bn H.Q. Parties from the 9/L/L Oke laid & took along the Bn front in preparation for the attack next morning.	STRICT
	2nd		On 1-30 A.M. the 9/R.G.F. Bat. less the 15 L.A.N.F.U.S. on the left, were formed up for the attack, the advance started at 1.55 A.M. the night was clear with a fairly bright moon. Neither our assault of that day was observed and the enemy put up lights at long distance at the same time firing rifle and M.G. and rifle fire. She enemy artillery was slow to open and were not shells falling behind our line. Our artillery did not fire until zero plus 8 minutes. Our BN was moved for counter attack, and at BHeat the artillery closed in their Coys ready to advance if called upon. Coys still more were around but from the troops in front and further were sent up by 'C' and 'D' Coys and brought his useful information. At 6½ morning it was known that the 11th A. Border Reg. were against on Coys 400 or 600 × to front, he S.O.S. was sent up by the troops on front with the Cars on their front. One dry front fairly quickly until 4.15 am, when the enemy came on with rifle and machine gun fire, and the S.O.S. was sent up by the troops on front. The news of the attack Maj Bryant were seen advancing in numbers from Brehn, and Ansks O'Cull to our advance. C + D Coys artillery were in the march of Brehn to advance; by our own quick fire the advance and good front with Kebris a good start under fairly heavy machine gun fire. Runners and Sergeants of 'A' Bn. HQ stated well formed with them. Our advance reached 400 × on the front of VIRILE FARM, and dug themselves in. On line those Fingers sent from VEX FARM on the right to about V.29.h.40,90, where it bent back to the middle lines. Our own attack did not get through our barrage as Stragglers + C.O's 97,04! Bys. came back and were collected for the defence of the favorite line and ordered to strengthen and defend the line	

WAR DIARY
or
INTELLIGENCE SUMMARY

(Erase heading not required.)

Army Form C. 2118

Place	Date	Hour	Summary of Events and Information	Remarks and references to Appendices
	1914 DEC.			
	2nd		During the night our men were withdrawn and regrouped in their respective units, and the	
	3rd		relief was carried out quietly and the Bn. made ready to act in support to the other battalions were consolidated. At night the Bn. was relieved by the 1st Bn. Dorset Regt. and moved back to IRISH FARM Casualties killed to line 2 other [Cakolds unknown] Lieut. SUTHERLAND, HARCOURT, STANHURST and DAVIDSON wounded. O.R. 23 K.i.A. 10 Missing. 88 Wounded.	
	4th		Bn. at IRISH FARM new drafts arrived and clearing up.	
	5th 6th to 12th 13th		Bn. performed routine duties — do —	
	14th		Bn. arrived into the line and relieved the 2nd B. R.Innis. Fus. Bn. HQ at HUENER FARM. The Bn first extended from the PADDEBEEK to the LEVERSTOTERBEEK at V.21.6.15.15 and holds the line of Doeman huts — (B Coy right, D Coy centre) the line was held by two Coys with A Coy in support — C Coy in reserve. The relief was effected without casualties. Nothing occurred on the same night.	
	15th		do — do — The trenches within the line were badly damaged by shellfire to the southward greatly so to the left of SOURD FARM. At night Orders were issued and at midnight units crossed the LEVENBOTZERBEEK and PADDEBEEK and commenced the formation of 200 by 300 w[ ] fire trenches. There were 600 yards in the line wasted. Shells 6 ft deep within [ ] was tasted to be worked [ ] were killed, Rollin, the sumuca [ ] and at night C Coy as[ ] the A Coy in to box at night within A 19 A.86.40.	
	16th		at night orders were issued for the positions V.29.d.65.50 – d.V.28.b.20.50 with the right to be line between V.29.c. d.29.A.80.40 C Coy with HQ at SOURD FARM. Relieved [ ] posts in[ ]	

WAR DIARY or INTELLIGENCE SUMMARY

Army Form C. 2118

1st to 31st December 1917   Sheet 3

Place	Date	Hour	Summary of Events and Information	Remarks and references to Appendices
	1917 Dec 16	cont	Got rations and set forth to get back with the least possible middle but found the Lads, but middle of the sea too the corner. "C" Coy's two lots remained out during the day, but rest of Coy was sent to relieve the guards on the right arrangements by the spleen of the 1st Can. Lancers. They were about to relieve the guard. On the night of 17/18, the Bn was relieved by the 3rd Bn 10th C.M.R. and moved by train to SIEGE CAMP. Assemble billets in the hut. HQR HQ A. & C. R. Wimereux.	Ref. Ops Oders by 15th Can Lancers, & his Bn A.H.Q. 181.
	17th		At SIEGE CAMP - Bn cleaning up	
	18		Brining the Coy arrangements, and outside working parties	
	19, 20		do	
	21		home leave	Lieut. W.G.H.J. Scully V.C. went on 14 days
	22		At SIEGE CAMP. Major D. LINDSAY took over temporary command of the Bn.	
	23		Bn relieved the 2nd Bn Monmouths Regt. on the YPRES CANAL BANK - Officers + OR on duty nits.	
	24		Bn working on the Coy's Defensive Areas.	
	25		Christmas Day Work carried on. No fires would or the works done. No Christmas festivities.	
	26-28		Working Parties on the Coy's Defensive Areas.	
	29		The Bn entrained at IRISH FARM (STEAM TRAM) at midday, being relieved by the 1st Bn K.R.R. and detrained at AUDRUICQ, at 5 PM. 1st Bn moved off at ST LOUIS H.Q. and "A" Coy to BILLES B, C, & D Coys in billets at ALEMBON by 11pm 29/12/17.	A.H.Z. ROULE SHEETS 7A CALAIS SHEET 13
	30		SANGHEM where detraining, B, C, & D Coys in billets at ALEMBON. A very trying march, as the roads were covered with ice and snow.	
	31		SUNDAY. Dr. Van made a church of some kind, all the Bn units which had come in late train arrived at 10 AM and the damaged units had travelled home arrived at 5 AM. Cleaning up and inspection parades.	

1st January 1918.

E. Lindsay, Major
O.C. 16th Bn Northumberland Fusiliers.

Confidential 96/31

WAR DIARY
of
16th Bn. Northumberland Fusiliers
1st to 31st January, 1918.

Vol. XXVI

WAR DIARY
or
INTELLIGENCE SUMMARY.

(Erase heading not required.)

Army Form C. 2118.

Place	Date	Hour	Summary of Events and Information	Remarks and references to Appendices
SANGHEN	1/1/18		Batt. billeted in SANGHEN and ALEMBON. Training.	MAP CALAIS 13.
	2/1/18		- do -	
	3/1/18		- do -	
	4/1/18		- do -	
	5/1/18		- do -	
	6/1/18		Sunday. Church Parade.	
	7/1/18		Training. Col. A.J. Tenby returned from leave. Major D. Tenby second in command.	
	8/1/18		Brigade Inspection cancelled owing to weather	
	9/1/18		Granted as a holiday by the Batt. in place of Christmas Day.	
	10/1/18		Training	
	11/1/18		- do -	
	12/1/18		- do -	
	13/1/18		Sunday. Church Parade.	
	14/1/18		Training.	
	15/1/18		- do -	
	16/1/18		- do - Major E. Thompson reported for duty.	
	17/1/18		- do - During the Batt's. stay at SANGHEN and ALEMBON the weather was very bad, frost & thaw alternating, the ground generally covered with snow.	

Army Form C. 2118

WAR DIARY
or
INTELLIGENCE SUMMARY
(Erase heading not required.)

Instructions regarding War Diaries and Intelligence Summaries are contained in F.S. Regs., Part II. and the Staff Manual respectively. Title Pages will be prepared in manuscript.

Place	Date	Hour	Summary of Events and Information	Remarks and references to Appendices
SANGHEN	18/1/18		The Batt. marched to LANDRETHUN. Billeted in village.	MAP CALAIS 13. SHEET 28.
	19/1/18		The Batt. marched to AUDRUICQ and entrained for ELVERDINGHE. Thence marched to DIRTY BUCKET CAMP. Billeted in huts.	
	20/1/18		Sunday. Church Parade.	
	21/1/18		In DIRTY BUCKET CAMP.	
	22/1/18		The Batt. moved to IRISH FARM	
	23/1/18		The Batt. worked on the Army Line. The C.O. reconnoitred the Army Defence Line.	
	24/1/18		- do -	
	25/1/18		The Batt. marched to EMILE CAMP, near ELVERDINGHE.	
	26/1/18		In EMILE CAMP.	
	27/1/18		Sunday. Church Parade.	
	28/1/18		The Batt. marched to BABOON CAMP	
	29/1/18		In BABOON CAMP.	
	30/1/18		In the evening the Batt. relieved the 2nd R. INNES. FUS on the right sector, the line running approximately from V.7.b.15/40. across the STADEN RY. at VIC 5050 to U.6.a.90/60. "B" Coy on right, "D" on left. "C" in support and "A" in reserve. Batt. HQ at EGYPT HOUSE. The relief was completed without casualties. While visiting the posts during the night Major Thompson was wounded by rifle fire at about V.7.a.70/70. Army Scout Okelly, his army machine gun orderly, was at first missed owing to the enemy cunning the day. No shelling, but moments later T.M. and M.G. activity at Major do. in the afternoon, but when the C/O "D" Coy was visiting the posts he ascertained that they 1st NCO and 2 men of No 9 Post were missing.	MAP A1. 1:10,000
	31/1/18			O'Scott 16th Nov 18 Lt Col 1st [illegible] 16 Nov 18

Confidential.

WA 27

War Diary.

of

16th Bn. Northumberland Fusiliers.

1st to 7th February 1918.

Volume XXVII.

WAR DIARY
or
INTELLIGENCE SUMMARY

Army Form C. 2118.

Place	Date	Hour	Summary of Events and Information	Remarks and references to Appendices
EGYPT HOUSE	1/2/18		Batt. holding the line on right sector, from approximately V7.6.15/40 across the STADEN RAILWAY to U6.d.90/60. In the evening an inter-company relief was carried out, "A" Company relieving "B" on the right and "C" Company relieving "D" on the left. During the night a Battle Patrol under 2nd LT. BROWNRIGG made a determined attack on an enemy post near TURENNE CROSSING and succeeded in entering the post, but the garrison had withdrawn to two Pill Boxes close at hand, from which a heavy fire was opened on the Patrol. A further attack on the Pill Boxes was attempted, but the fire was too close & accurate, & the Patrol withdrew with the loss of two killed and one wounded. Unsuccessful attempt to bring back.	MAP A1. 1:10000
	2/2/18		At night a Battle Patrol under LT. WATTS attacked an enemy post in front of the left Company but was met by heavy machine gun fire & forced to withdraw with a loss of one O.R. killed, one missing believed killed and three wounded. Other patrols under 2nd LT. BROWN were out on the night. Ł 1/2 & V.20/7.40 the aim not succeed in getting into touch with the enemy who was very alert & kept his machine guns active.	
ABRI CAMP	3/2/18		At night the Batt. was relieved by the 16th LANC. FUSILIERS, and moved back. "B" and "D" Companies to the CORPS LINE and "A" & "C" Companies and HeadQuarters to ABRI CAMP.	
	4/2/18		In the afternoon "A" and "C" Companies relieved "B" and "D" Companies in the CORPS LINE.	

Army Form C. 2118

WAR DIARY
or
INTELLIGENCE SUMMARY
(Erase heading not required.)

Instructions regarding War Diaries and Intelligence Summaries are contained in F. S. Regs, Part II. and the Staff Manual respectively. Title Pages will be prepared in manuscript.

Place	Date	Hour	Summary of Events and Information	Remarks and references to Appendices
ABRI CAMP	5/7/18		The Batt. was relieved by the 5/6th ROYAL SCOTS & moved back to LARRY CAMP.	
LARRY CAMP	6/7/18		The Batt. paraded & was inspected by the G.O.C. 32nd Division and the G.O.C. 96th Inf. Brigade.	
	7/7/18		The Batt. was inspected. "A" Company went to the 1/4th, "B" to the 1/5th, "C" to the 1/6th and "D" to the 1/7th Northumberland Fus. Batt. of fairly & a few H.Q. officers and other ranks remained behind.	

O. Scully Lt/Col
Comdg 16th Northd Fus.

www.ingramcontent.com/pod-product-compliance
Lightning Source LLC
Chambersburg PA
CBHW081537160426

43191CB00011B/1783